UNIVERSE, EARTH, HUMAN BEING

UNIVERSE, EARTH, HUMAN BEING

IN THEIR RELATIONSHIP TO EGYPTIAN MYTHS AND MODERN CIVILIZATION

Eleven lectures given in Stuttgart between 4 and 16 August 1908

INTRODUCTION BY MARIE STEINER

RUDOLF STEINER

RUDOLF STEINER PRESS

CW 105

Rudolf Steiner Press
Hillside House, The Square
Forest Row, RH18 5ES

www.rudolfsteinerpress.com

Published by Rudolf Steiner Press 2022

Originally published in German under the title *Welt, Erde, Mensch, deren Wesen und Entwickelung sowie ihre Spiegelung in dem Zusammenhang zwischen ägyptischem Mythol und gegenwärtiger Kultur* (volume 105 in the *Rudolf Steiner Gesamtausgabe* or Collected Works) by Rudolf Steiner Verlag, Dornach. Based on shorthand notes that were not reviewed or revised by the speaker

Published by permission of the Rudolf Steiner Nachlassverwaltung, Dornach

Edited translation revised by Matthew Barton

A catalogue record for this book is available from the British Library

ISBN 978 1 85584 602 9

Cover by Morgan Creative
Typeset by Symbiosys Technologies, Vishakapatnam, India
Printed and bound by 4Edge Ltd., Essex

CONTENTS

Publisher's Note

Although dated in certain respects and dealing to some degree with historical conflicts, the bulk of Marie Steiner's original Introduction to this volume is included here, reflecting with passion and fervour her summation of anthroposophy and the context of the lectures transcribed in this volume.

From 1906 on, Rudolf Steiner began to present entire lecture cycles outside of Berlin. After Paris and Leipzig, a course followed in Stuttgart in August 1906 under the title: 'Vor dem Tore der Theosophie' (GA 95, published in English as *Founding a Science of the Spirit*). The second cycle held in Stuttgart was the present one.

In the original German publication of these lectures, Marie Steiner commented as follows:

> Over 300 members of the Theosophical Society responded to this call, and for many of them this cycle of lectures has become the most significant event of their lives. Enormous, cosmic pictures were unfolded before the spiritual gaze of the listeners, insights were into such depths of ancient wisdom, views of distant futures of the development of mankind and the world, human and world development, that deepest devotion must have flowed through listeners' hearts and a joyful, powerful expectancy of the future could fill their souls, in conscious recognition of the great task that has been given to mankind on this earth.
>
> Those who were able to stay in the circle of our dear Stuttgart friends on those unforgettable days, which were so rich in significant impressions, will recall that time with grateful feelings, which are first and foremost directed to our venerated teacher, but then to the Stuttgart friends who made such a meeting possible for us.
>
> It was also of special value for the members who had come from other branches to gain an insight into the way in which work is done in

the Stuttgart branches. Opportunity for this was given by the beautiful esoteric lectures of Miss Toni Völker, who gave intimate insights into the path of the esoteric pupil, and by the interesting lectures of Dr Carl Unger, who approached the theosophical teachings more in a scientific sense. What came to light most of all was the agreement and harmony which in truth prevails between these two seemingly so different orientations; this was especially expressed where the scientific explanations flowed into the path of pupilship. In their entirety, these lectures have shown how pure thought and esotericism can perfectly complement each other.

Introduction

This cycle of lectures now published in book form was given by Rudolf Steiner in 1908. The following words of his might well serve as its motto: 'The mission of our age is not to reproduce an ancient wisdom, but engender a new wisdom, one that points not only to the past but that works prophetically into the future.'

The previous year, at the memorable congress of the General Theosophical Society in Munich,[1] Rudolf Steiner clearly outlined what was needed to revive the theosophical movement, at that time at risk of succumbing to the influence of Oriental ideas which did not meet contemporary needs.

In contrast to the many grievous misunderstandings that had arisen, Rudolf Steiner's teaching offered something positive for the growth of humanity. On that occasion, too, he first gave artistic expression to his spiritual teaching. The colours of the walls and the pictures of the seals embodied Rosicrucian spiritual aims: the motifs of the columns conveyed our evolutionary future, and this was aided by the performance of *The Sacred Drama of Eleusis* by Édouard Schuré, which presented the mysteries of Ancient Greece in a living way. Rudolf Steiner connected these with the mythology of northern Germany. He had something new to give which hitherto had not been available to followers of an Anglo-Indian theosophy.

The courage with which Rudolf Steiner trod new paths stirred up spiritual opposition among the leaders of the Theosophical Society, who sought constantly to hamper and fetter him. This opposition forced him to withdraw from the post he had held in the Society. The conditions under which he had undertaken office were these: that he should be free, through a Western esotericism, to allow what shed light on the mystery of Christ to flow into European culture. When certain leading theosophical circles recognized the remarkable spiritual capacities and the knowledge that Rudolf Steiner was able to bring to bear on this problem, means were sought to hamper his activity. They considered that the best way to do this was to proclaim the coming of Christ again in the flesh, in the body of a Hindu boy, and quiet preparations were made for the appearance a few years later of Krishnamurti as a future world teacher.

It was whispered that the appearance of Krishnamurti would compel Rudolf Steiner to divulge Christian secrets concerning which he would ordinarily have been silent. This interfered with his quiet and steady aim in building up the system and organization of his teachings. He considered it his task to instruct humanity in the methods of initiation suited to modern conditions of consciousness. Beside the reverent pursuit of ancient wisdom, it was necessary to waken an understanding of the changed form in which this wisdom was now to be given, and to show how such forms are subject to a continual emergence, maturation and decline, in order that new life may spring ever and again from what is dead. An historical sense had to be aroused in people, not merely a wonder-filled contemplation of ancient revelations. The mysterious connection of the great cosmic laws uniting one age of civilization with another had to be made known. No one had ever described in so powerful and sublime a fashion the primeval wisdom which streamed down to earth from spiritual heights as Rudolf Steiner had done. No one before him had been able to speak in terms appropriate to modern consciousness of the reflection of universal cosmic existence in the human individual —the microcosm.

All this teaching culminated in the central event of human evolution: the descent of the sun spirit into the body of Jesus of Nazareth. Rudolf Steiner showed how the sun forces were thereby able to penetrate and spiritualize the planet, summoning humankind to fit itself for the task before it. By the death on Golgotha an incisive mystic reality was consummated; it was a unique, unrepeatable event, for otherwise it would have taken place in vain.

In order that these truths might be brought to humanity, fact by fact had to be introduced in gently balanced stages. The foundations had already been laid before Krishnamurti was presented. In this cycle, in the year 1908, Rudolf Steiner had already embarked upon the path, describing the consistent sequence of events from civilization to civilization and illuminating the great central event. There are occasions when the time in which a truth is to be proclaimed may be hastened; it may be necessary to confront certain challenges with facts which one would rather have allowed to speak for themselves. This does not mean that something was done which otherwise would not have been done; it had to be done because it was rooted in the deepest necessities of contemporary evolution, both cosmic and human. With complete self-sacrifice, therefore, Rudolf Steiner assumed this responsibility as his life's task. The Theosophical Society cut itself off from this influx of new wisdom, it rejected what would have infused new life into it, which would have enhanced admiring recognition of an ancient, honoured wisdom with new, historical meaning. If it had instead engaged with what was presented, the Theosophical Society would have been led from the ripened wisdom of India by way of Persia, Chaldea and Egypt, deeply into the mystery of the 'chosen people'—chosen for a reason that would have become intelligible; and thence it would have been led to the mystery places of Asia Minor and southern Europe. Further, these teachings would have shed light on the soul-life of the expectant peoples of Central and Northern Europe and would have culminated in the event of Golgotha, when the hitherto hidden and veiled mysteries stepped forth on to the scene of world history.

Every individual evolves within the general evolution of humanity, and all must learn to find within themselves their central purpose, which is primarily in spiritual experience. The tragedy of the individual personality lies in its severance from the spiritual world; in its seeking, erring and striving within the approaching night of separation from what is spiritual, through to its tragic fate in the darkness of materialism. Comprehension of such things is necessary if we are to understand ourselves. Into this night of darkness shines a light, the light of Christian esotericism which was kindled in Palestine and passed thence into Europe. It broke with wonderful clarity over the island of Hibernia, where, notwithstanding the repression of the monastic colonies by a Church fettered by Roman imperialism, its radiance endured in secret as a stream of spiritual force.

Through this there arose the spiritual orders of knighthood and the desire for religious communities. German mysticism appeared as a rich blossom of deep religious fervour. In order to keep pace with events, above all with the conquests of science, and in order that faith might stand firm in the darkness of a materialistic age, something further had to emerge. The power of belief had to yield to the certainty of science. This was the task of the Rosicrucian schools. They concerned themselves with the newly evolving forces of consciousness in the coming age. Rosicrucian esotericism, with its earnest striving for the new forces of human knowledge, with the tragic fate and spiritual tests laid upon its followers, was yet able here and there, as Rudolf Steiner has shown us, to raise the veil of its mysteries. New forces of spiritual consciousness were born from it that were able to overcome materialism through powers of cognition.

In the hard struggle to recover the faculty of spiritual perception, once given to humankind and now lost, but needing to be regained through the power of the I, through the death and rebirth of the personality, the I-being of striving humanity grows strong. When we consciously grasp this I-being we can rise and unite ourselves once more with the godhead. The divine I descended—once—to earth so that this might come to pass. The unique character of this event must be recognized as the decisive turning point of the earth's destiny. Rosicrucian teaching sums it up in the motto '*In Christo Morimur*': in Christ we die to live above, to live upwards to the spirit. '*Per Spiritum Sanctum Reviviscimus*': through striving towards the Christ we gain true life, we become awake in the spirit out of which we once were born.

The individual personality had to come into being, it had to comprehend itself, to take itself in hand and recognize itself as a centre, be horrified by itself, confront and then overcome itself, to learn to die, that it might realize itself again as a free I-being whose central point is the divine I. This is the path of Western esotericism; we cannot avoid it. Formerly our task was to take in hand the education of the personality, entangled as it was in egoism; our present task is to overcome egoism, to transmute it by liberating the divine-devoted, strong I-nature within us. This we can only do by mastering the forces of our consciousness through knowledge and cognition. We must be willing to recognize the smallest in the greatest. We cannot ignore whole epochs of time with their tremendous significance for human evolution. Power will be given to us if today we seek knowledge of the universe, earth and the human being.

This knowledge is now called anthroposophy. It gives its teaching and declares its creed quite openly; it hides nothing, for it knows the time has come when what was once nurtured in secret must step forth on to the plane of history. In describing the descent of the human being from the divine and our way back to it again, anthroposophy might have felt secure within genuine theosophy, for they are so far one and the same: '*Ex Deo Nascimur*'—out of God we are born, and to the godhead we return when we have received the Christ unto us.

Let us close these observations with words of Rudolf Steiner:

> We see a primeval wisdom preserved in the mysteries of past epochs; but our wisdom must be an apocalyptic wisdom, whose seeds we must plant. We have need once again of a principle of initiation in which our original connection with the spiritual world can be re-established.

This is the task of the anthroposophic world movement.

Marie Steiner
1930

Lecture 1

STUTTGART, 4 AUGUST 1908

The Egyptian Period and the Present Time

THE first lecture of this course will offer, by way of introduction, an outline of the subject before us. We shall not enter fully into this yet, but will first give an outline of things we shall speak of during the next few days. We have a very extensive theme before us: the universe, the earth, and the human being, and I propose to give a brief survey of all the knowledge we can acquire about visible and invisible worlds.

Our feelings are borne into the farthest distance of the cosmos when, in the deepest and most worthy sense, we employ the word 'universe'. 'Earth' indicates the field of action upon which humanity is now placed, upon which we are to work and live, and whose mission we seek to understand. Lastly, the word 'man' or 'human being'—a word we here wish to understand in its esoteric sense—indicates what the mystics of all ages meant when they made use of the expression, 'O man, know thyself!'[2]

We also have a subtitle to our subject. Having set ourselves such an important task, this subtitle is in a certain way justified; for when we consider the connection between that wonderful pre-Christian civilization—the Egyptian—and our own, we see how mysterious are the forces permeating human life. Three ages of human endeavour and enquiry, of human evolution, morality, and life, rise before us when we consider Egyptian civilization and that of our own day. When we speak of Egyptian civilization in the esoteric sense we mean the civilization that had its seat in the north-east of Africa, on the banks of the Nile, which lasted for thousands of years and ended in the eighth century before Christ. We know that this civilization was followed by another which we call the Greco-Roman. This was centred on the one hand in the wonderful Greek race, with their highly cultivated sense of beauty, and on the other hand in the powerful state of Rome. We also know that in this age occurred the mighty event in earthly evolution which we recognize as the advent of Christ Jesus. Then followed the epoch in which we are now living.

First the Egyptian epoch with all that belonged to it—and a great deal belonged to it—then the Greco-Roman era with its great fruits—the rise of Christianity—and then our present age. These are the three ages which come before our mind's eye when we consider the subtitle of these lectures.

One of the things we will study is the interplay of mysterious forces between the age of civilization first mentioned and our own. It is as if in the Egyptian age certain seeds were sown in the breast of gradually developing humanity, seeds which remained hidden during the Greco-Roman age and have reappeared in a particular manner in the present. Much of what buds in our souls today, much of what surrounds us, and of which people speak and dream, has sprung like a seed from ancient Egyptian civilization without people being aware of it.

You are all more or less acquainted with the telegraphic apparatus. You know that wires connecting the different apparatuses extend from one place to another, and without having any deep knowledge of these things you understand that the force which sets the apparatus in motion has something to do with the energy which flows through the wires. You perhaps also know that there is a connection down in the earth, that the ends of the wires are connected with the earth; but this subterranean connection is invisible because it is made by more or less mysterious forces produced by the earth itself. Something similar exists as a deep mystery in the evolution of the human being. In history we see threads being spun which lie within the invisible world. By means of history and of esotericism we can trace what took place in Ancient Egypt. We see how the threads of culture stretch from the Greek age, the Roman, the Christian, down into our own age. All these are guided by a kind of connection that takes place above the earth, but there is also a hidden, a subterranean force which works more or less directly from the Ancient Egyptian age into our own. Many a remarkable secret is revealed to us when we trace these connections and examine them thoroughly.

To begin with I shall indicate briefly the particular realities referred to in the subtitle of our theme. When we look back to Ancient Egypt and observe a few of the mighty records there we are struck by the Pyramids, for example, and also the Sphinx—that wonderful and enigmatic figure. Then we let our glance pass on to Ancient Greece. Here the Greek temple appears with its unique architecture. We can see and admire what we know from history of this wonderful land; we see its sculptures, those great, ideal, and perfect human forms described as gods: Zeus, Demeter, Pallas Athene, Apollo. Then we turn to the ancient kingdom of the Romans. Something remarkable appears when we thus allow our vision to sweep from the ancient Grecian peninsula to the Italian. Before us appear the forms of Ancient Rome, many of which are still preserved; we see figures clothed with the toga, which is indeed more than a mere outer dress. What do we feel with regard to these Roman figures? One might say regarding certain of those figures of the Roman Republic that it is as if the ideal forms of the Greeks had descended from their pedestals and had appeared before us as people of flesh and blood. What we behold is their inner power; we recognize what lies in this inner power when we compare what developed in Ancient Rome with the feeling, the thought, the content of a figure belonging to the Grecian States—that of a Spartan or an Athenian, for example. We feel what this figure contains. People belonging to Sparta or Athens felt that they were first of all Spartans or Athenians. Belonging in a certain way and to a certain degree to a common soul, the Spartan or Athenian felt more what we might call the Greek *polis* than his own personality; he felt himself more as a Spartan or as an Athenian, than as an individual human citizen; he felt that the power working so strongly in him proceeded more from the common spirit of the people than from his own personal power. The Roman on the contrary appears to us as being centred more directly upon his own personality. Hence in the Roman kingdom there appears something very special, namely an understanding of the rights of the citizen. All that legal scholars nowadays dream about the origin of 'justice' prior to this is very different from what in times of better understanding was rightly called 'Roman Law'.

In Ancient Rome human beings learned to regard themselves as individuals, they stood upon their own two feet, no longer belonging merely to a certain city-state, but Roman citizens; that is to say they felt themselves centred in their own human nature. With this feeling of individuality the time had arrived when what was spiritual in each human being descended to earth. Previously it was perceived as hovering, so to speak, above him in spiritual regions. There is something unique in Roman law and in Roman civilization. Let us consider the circumstance that the Greek felt himself primarily to be a Spartan or an Athenian. What was the spirit of Athens or of Sparta? For us anthroposophists this was no abstraction, but something like a spiritual cloud, which in its turn was the spiritual expression of a spiritual being in which the town of Athens or Sparta was embedded; but this being was not visible upon the physical plane. The Greek looked primarily not to himself, but to something above him, the Roman looked primarily to himself. It was he who first recognized the human being as the highest creature that can take on fleshly form upon the physical plane. The spirit had come completely down into humankind. This was the time when the divine itself could descend into human evolution and incarnate in Jesus Christ.

The manner in which Egyptian civilization extended into the Greco-Roman age was a very wonderful process. When higher realms entrusted Moses, in Egypt, with leading his people to the 'One God', we recall that he asked God, 'What shall I say to my people when they ask who sent me?' And God answered (and we shall see what deep truth lay hidden in the statement): 'Say to those to whom I send thee, "I AM" hath sent me unto you.' Thus 'I AM' is the name of an individual God who worked and ruled at that time as the Christ principle in spiritual heights, and who had not yet descended to the physical plane. To whom did this voice belong which could make itself perceptible to the initiate Moses, saying to him, as it were from spiritual worlds, 'I am the "I AM"'?[3] It was the very same being (and this is the secret of the ancient Greek mysteries) who appeared later in the flesh as the Christ: only afterwards was he visible to those around him, while previously he could speak only through initiates from spiritual heights.

Thus we see the deity—the spiritual principle—gradually descending after humanity had been prepared, after it had learnt in the Roman age the importance of embodiment in the flesh and its manifestation on the physical plane. We see how a whole series of the results of civilization develop in an exceedingly profound way from what the human being received as a new gift at that time. We see how the form of the Pyramids and the temple change to that of the Romanesque church—another record of inner human creative work. We see how from the sixth century the Cross with the dead Jesus makes its appearance; and how by degrees out of the stream of Christianity a remarkable figure evolves whose mysteries are very deeply veiled. We need only call up this figure before our eyes in the wonderful form given to it by the painter's art in the *Sistine Madonna*, by Raphael.

Everyone knows this wonderful figure of the Virgin in the centre of the picture, carrying the child in her arms, and we have certainly all felt a corresponding emotional thrill when confronted by it. I would ask you, however, to note one thing with regard to it which expresses the spiritual striving of humanity at the stage with which we are dealing—the three civilizations mentioned above. It is not for nothing that the artist has surrounded the Madonna with a cloud from which emerge a great number of similar little children, a crowd of angelic forms.

Let us now allow our feeling to be completely absorbed by this picture of the Madonna. Anyone whose emotion is sufficiently deep for them to be able to do this will feel and perceive that there is something very different here from what an ordinary, mundane intellect will see in the picture. Do these cloud-angels surrounding the Madonna not say something to us? Yes, they say something of the greatest significance if we only consider them deeply enough. When we allow ourselves to sink deeply into this picture, something whispers in our soul, 'Here before us is a miracle in the best sense of the word.' We do not think that this child whom the Madonna bears in her arms is born in the ordinary way from the woman. No! These wonderfully delicate angel-forms we see in the clouds seem to be in process of development, and the child in the Madonna's arms seems to be only a more condensed manifestation of them, like something that had crystallized somewhat more than these fleeting angel-forms, which seems as if brought down from the clouds and held fast in her arms. It is thus this child appears to us, and not as if born from the woman. We are directed to a mysterious connection between the child and the virgin mother. If we call up the picture thus before our souls, another virgin mother appears to our mental vision: the ancient Egyptian Isis, with the child Horus, and we may become aware of a mysterious connection between the Christian Madonna and the Egyptian figure on whose temple were written the words, 'I AM that which is, and was, and is to come; my veil no mortal can raise.'[4]

What we have hinted at as a miracle in the picture of the Madonna is also revealed in the Egyptian myth, for it there describes Horus as not having been born through conception, but tells how a beam of light fell from Osiris upon Isis, a kind of miraculous birth took place, and the child Horus appeared. Here again we see how threads connect one thing with another; what we are here able to investigate is without any earthly connection.

Let us now pass on to where our own age begins. Let us think of the Gothic cathedral with its wondrous construction of pointed arches; let us call to mind what took place there in the Middle Ages, in gatherings where true believers met true priests. Think of the effect of this Gothic cathedral with its many-coloured panes of glass through which the sunlight penetrates; consider how many of those who were able to speak of the deeper secrets of the world's evolution could let resound tones whose outward reflection was the wonderful light split thus into varied colours. Again and again it happened that the priests showed how the common power of the divine being was imparted to humanity in separate rays of power, refracted like the light which streamed in through the coloured windows. The division or refraction of the light was placed before human senses, and in their souls was aroused what spiritually underlay this symbol.

In this way the Gothic cathedral pervaded worshippers' powers of perception and feeling.

Let us now enter more deeply into what is thus inwardly pictured. Let us first consider the Egyptian Pyramid—a most characteristic form of architecture! We must exert ourselves to discover what it has to say to us. By degrees we shall see how in the Pyramid, the secret of the universe, the earth and the human being is expressed; we shall see that it expresses what the Egyptian priest felt in the service of his religion. Later we shall penetrate deeply into all these things; today we will only notice what such a priest felt, and imparted to his people in pictures. The wisdom expressed in the Egyptian form of religion was very profound; it was the direct result of ancient tradition, like a memory, and the Egyptian sage in his meeting with Solon could say with truth: 'You Greeks remain children all your lives, and in your childish souls is none of the ancient truth!' Whence came this wisdom to which reference is here made?[5]

Our present humanity was preceded, as you know, by another which dwelt upon a continent over which the billows of the Atlantic Ocean now roll. When the great Atlantean flood took place, the knowledge of the Atlanteans was carried towards the East across what is today Europe. The northern myths have remained behind as memories of the wisdom of Atlantis. We know that the successors of the Atlanteans carried the wisdom of Ancient India and Persia into Asia. We also know that Egyptian wisdom was partly reanimated by Asia, but that it also streamed directly from the West, from Atlantis, towards Africa.

Now what sort of wisdom was it that was referred to by the ancient sage when he spoke of the 'ancient truth'? This will be disclosed if for a moment we pause to consider the difference between life today and life in Ancient Atlantis. At that time the human being was gifted with a dim clairvoyance; around him he saw beings who are also around us today, but whom present-day humankind sees no longer. The earth contains not only plants, minerals, and animals; spiritual beings also surround us, but these are visible only to clairvoyant eyes. In Atlantis at that time human beings were clairvoyant as a matter of course; divine beings were their companions: they lived with them as we now live with other human beings. There was not as yet that sharp distinction between day-consciousness and night-consciousness that now exists. At the present time, when our astral body and I enter into physical life in the morning, physical objects surround us; and when at night we rise out of our physical body, this world becomes dark and dim to us. This is the case today in normal human beings; but in Atlantis it was not so, particularly in its earliest periods. When at night people emerged from their physical and etheric body, darkness did not then spread around them; they entered a world of spiritual beings and saw these divine spiritual forms just as they now sees corporeal forms. They saw Baldur, Wotan, Zeus, and Apollo—who are not imaginary, fanciful figures, but are the expression of real beings who, at the time of which we are speaking, had not taken on bodies of flesh, but possessed, as their densest form, transparent etheric bodies. When people of those times withdrew from their physical body at night, these beings surrounded them as etheric forms; and when in the morning they again drew into their physical body they were in the world of reality which today is for them the only world. They left for a time, one might say, the world of the gods, and dipped down into the world of physical, corporeal existence. There was no strict boundary between their day perception and night perception, and when in those times the initiate spoke to ordinary people of these divine beings he was not speaking of something that was strange to them. It was the same as when we speak of people today and call them by their names: the initiate spoke of such beings as Wotan and Baldur, knowing them as divine, etheric beings.

The memory of that ancient wisdom and of these experiences was carried with them by those who journeyed towards the East; and these memories were connected with something else which developed in the singular constitution of the Egyptian people—the conviction that an eternal spiritual part dwells in us, and that when our body becomes a corpse it has been forsaken by this divine, spiritual part. This conviction is expressed in numerous symbols and teachings which the Egyptian priests gave to the people; it was not merely an abstract truth to them, it was a truth in which they lived, and which they experienced directly.

Let us describe what the Egyptian perceived. He said, 'I see here a corpse, the dust of the human being who was the bearer of an I; I know—for I know it from ancient tradition and from the experience of my ancestors—that there is something else, a spiritual part, which passes into other worlds. This could not fulfil its task were it to live solely in that spiritual world. A connecting link must be formed between this spiritual part and the earthly world; we must form a magnetic link for the soul which passes at death into higher realms, in order to arouse in it a feeling of permanence, so that it may return again, and appear once more on this earth.'

We know from the teachings of spiritual science that humanity itself ensures that the soul shall return again and again to new incarnations; we know that when human beings pass at death into other spheres, during the period in kamaloka (during which they wean themselves from what is earthly), they are still chained by certain forces to what is physical. We know that it is these forces which do not allow them to rise at once into the regions of devachan, and also draw them down again to a new incarnation. But we are a people today who live in abstractions, and who represent such things as theories. In Ancient Egypt all this lived as tradition. The Egyptian was the reverse of a theorist or mere thinker; he wanted to see with his senses how the soul took its way from the dead body into higher realms, he wanted to have this fashioned before him. These thoughts he embodied in the Pyramids: the way the soul rises, how it leaves the body, how it is still partly fettered, and how it is led upwards to higher regions. In the architecture of the Pyramids we can see the fettering of the soul to what is earthly; we can see how kamaloka with its mysterious forms comes before us, and we can say that, considered externally, it is a symbol of the soul which has left the body and is rising into higher realms.

Let us endeavour to understand these ancient traditions. In the Atlantean age human beings still saw around them much that is completely hidden from them today. You will recall from previous lectures that in Atlantis the human etheric body was not so intimately bound up with the physical body as it is now: the etheric head projected far beyond the physical head. In animals this formation has remained to the present day. When one observes a horse clairvoyantly, the etheric head may be seen towering upwards as a form of light above the horse's nose; and in the case of an elephant a truly remarkable structure can be seen above the trunk. In Atlantean humanity the etheric head was in a somewhat similar position, although not extending quite so far outwards. Later it gradually drew more and more into the physical head, so that now it is about the same size as the latter. On this account the physical head—which was at first only partly governed by the etheric head and still had many forces outside which are today within it—was not yet human-like to any great degree; it was only evolving, and still possessed a somewhat lower animal form.

What did the Atlantean see when he looked at a companion during the day? He saw a human being with a very receding forehead, very protruding teeth—something that reminded him of an animal; but at night when he slept and clairvoyant consciousness began, the animal-like form became less distinct, and out of the physical head grew the etheric head, which already had a human form and indeed a very much more beautiful form than we see today. In still more remote times the Atlantean clairvoyant could look back to a period when the human physical form was yet more animal-like though it possessed an etheric body that was entirely human; far more beautiful indeed than the present physical form, which has adapted itself to coarser, denser forces. Now imagine this memory of the Atlantean placed consciously yet symbolically before the people of Egypt. Imagine the Egyptian priest saying to the people: 'In Atlantean times your own souls, when you were awake, beheld the human figure with an animal form, but at night there grew out of it an exceedingly beautiful human head.' This memory, presented in sculpture, is the Sphinx. It is only thus that these forms can be understood; we must realize that they are not merely imagined forms, but realities.

Let us now pass from the Egyptian Pyramid to the Greek temple. These temples will only be understood by those who are able to sense that there are forces which govern space. The Greek possessed this feeling. Anyone studying space from the standpoint of spiritual science knows that it is not the absolute void of which our ordinary mathematicians and physicists dream, but that it is differentiated, structured. It is filled with lines, with lines of force in this direction and in that, from above downwards, from right to left, straight and curved lines going in every direction. Space may be felt, it may be penetrated with feeling. Those who have such a feeling for space know why certain old painters could paint the floating angel forms in pictures of the Madonna in a way so wonderfully true to nature; they know that these angels mutually sustain each other, just as the planets do in space by their power of attraction. It is quite different when we consider Böcklin's picture *Piety*.[6] Nothing is said here against the excellence of this picture otherwise, but anyone who has preserved the living feeling for space has the sensation that those remarkable angel forms might fall at any moment. The painters of olden times had the perception that belonged to earlier clairvoyance. In modern times this has been lost.

When art still possessed esoteric traditions, people acknowledged these mutually sustaining forces existing in space, streaming hither and thither. Such forces were perceived by those in whose minds the thought of the Greek temple originated. They did not think out these forms, but they perceived the forces streaming through space, and filled them with stone; what was already there invisibly they filled with substance. Hence the Greek temple is a material presentation of actual forces existing in space; a Greek temple is a crystallized space-thought in the purest sense of the word. The result of this was very important; by giving material expression to force forms in space, the Greeks gave divine spiritual beings the opportunity of using these material forms. It is no figure of speech but a fact when we say that gods came down at that time into the Greek temples in order to be among human beings on the physical plane.

Just as today parents furnish the child with a physical form, the corporeal body, in order that the spirit can express itself on the physical plane, so something similar took place in the case of the Greek temple. The opportunity was provided for divine spiritual beings to stream down and incarnate in the architectural structure. That is the secret of the Greek temple. God was present in the temple. Those who rightly experienced the form of the Greek temple felt that there need be no human being anywhere near it, nor in the temple itself, and yet it would not be empty, for the god was really present there. The Greek temple is a whole; it is complete in itself, because it has a form which magically draws the god into it.

If we now consider a Romanesque church, especially one with a crypt, we shall see a further development. In the Pyramid figures the path the soul takes after death presents the outer architectural form for the soul when departing; the Greek temple is the expression of the divine soul which likes to dwell upon the physical plane. The Romanesque church with its crypt corresponds to the Cross upon which the dead body of Jesus hangs. Humanity at this stage had progressed to an advanced consciousness in spiritual spheres. Whereas the Pyramids represent the bond with what is earthly, the period in kamaloka, the Cross expresses victory over the physical form, the victory over death, and reminds us of the spiritual victory of Christ over death.

Again, a further step is taken to the Gothic cathedral. Without the pious congregation within, it is incomplete. If we wish to feel it as a whole, then to the pointed arches must be added the folded hands and the upward-streaming feelings they express; not such feelings as are embodied in the crypt, which preserves the memory of the spiritual victory over death, but victorious feelings, such as the soul perceives who already in the body has felt that it is victorious over death. The soul, victorious over death while in the body, belongs to the Gothic building, which is incomplete if it is not filled with such feelings.

The Greek temple is the body of the god; it is complete in itself. The Gothic church is something which requires a congregation; it is not a temple but a *Dom*, a cathedral. The [German word] 'Dom' appears in the [English] suffix 'dom' in the words 'kingdom', 'Christendom', for example. It also lies at the root of the Russian word 'Duma'. A dome, or *Dom*, is something in which individual members are gathered together into one congregation. From this we can see how in time human thought and human perception progresses from the Pyramid to the Greek temple, then to the Romanesque church with its crypt, and afterwards to the Gothic cathedral.

Thus we arrive gradually at our own age, and we shall see how the forces of evolution are at work not only on the surface, but that mysterious underlying esoteric currents are also active, so that what is taking place today in our civilization appears as a re-embodiment of much that was sown within humanity in ancient Egyptian times.

We will close with a thought which hints at this mysterious connection. What constitutes the materialism of our present civilization? What is the special characteristic of human beings who, when they wish to see something spiritual, have lost the harmony that reconciles faith and knowledge? They see nothing! They regard the gross, material, physical part of the world as reality, even denying what is spiritual. They believe that our existence is over when our corpse lies in the earth; they see nothing rising up into the spiritual worlds. Can a conception such as this be the outcome of something that was sown at a time when there was a firm faith in the continued life of the soul, such as existed in Egypt? Yes, for in civilization things are not as in the vegetable kingdom, where like springs forth again from like. In civilization one characteristic alternates with another which is apparently dissimilar to it—and yet there may be deeper and more intimate similarities.

Perception of the human being is confined today to the physical body; people regard this as a reality; they cannot raise themselves to what is spiritual. The souls who now regard their physical bodies with their eyes, and are unable to rise to what is spiritual, were incarnated among earlier peoples as Greeks, as Romans, and as ancient Egyptians. All that exists in our souls today is the result of what we acquired in previous incarnations. Imagine your soul back in its Egyptian body. Imagine your soul after death being led up again by way of the Pyramid into higher spheres—but your body held fast as a mummy. This fact had an occult result. The soul always had to look downward when its mummified body was below; its thoughts were hardened, solidified, they were attracted to the physical world. It was forced to look down from the realms of the spirit upon its embalmed physical body, and in consequence the thought became rooted in it that the physical body had a higher reality than it actually had. Imagine a human soul looking down at that time upon its mummy. Thought regarding the physical hardened; it passed through repeated incarnations, and now is such that human beings cannot extricate their thoughts from the physical bodily form. Materialistic thought often results from this embalming of the body. Thus we see how thoughts and feelings work from one incarnation to another; how civilizations are perpetuated through repeated incarnations, and how they reappear later in entirely different forms. This ought to arouse a faint idea of the countless occult threads which are hidden below the surface.

In this lecture we have indicated briefly the subjects to be dealt with in subsequent lectures. In them our vision shall sweep upwards to the highest regions of those worlds beheld by the Egyptian priests; we shall have to direct our attention to the nature, the goal, and the destiny of the human being; and we shall understand how such problems as these are solved when we realize that the fruits of one age of civilization reappear in a wonderful and mysterious manner in a subsequent one.

Lecture 2

STUTTGART, 5 AUGUST 1908

Ancient Wisdom and the New Apocalyptic Wisdom

We shall enter best into our subject if in the first place we try to form a clear conception of the two extremes which have to be considered when we relate the universe to the human being. These two extremes are that of the spirit-soul and physical matter. We will endeavour to discuss these, starting with a phenomenon which is more or less of a riddle for people today, but which is found in the ancient Egyptian conception of the world and life. I mean what is called the 'temple sleep'.

The unique fact underlying the temple sleep is that among the Egyptian priests, and in ancient civilizations in general, wisdom was held to be very closely bound up with the art of healing and with health. The human being of today has only a dim conception of those ancient ideas about the inner relationships between wisdom and health, between science and the art of healing; and it will be the task of the anthroposophic movement to lead humanity once more to a conception of the spiritual through which wisdom and the art of healing can become closely connected once again. This recalls what was said in the last lecture, and that ancient figure we were reminded of when we looked at the picture of Raphael's *Madonna and Child*: of Isis with the child Horus, the goddess on whose temple were inscribed the words: 'I AM who was, who is, who will be; my veil no mortal can raise.' This goddess was mysteriously connected with the art of healing; she was regarded as the teacher of the Egyptian priesthood in this respect. There are remarkable sayings from the latter days of antiquity that show how Isis was particularly interested in the health of mankind at the time when she was placed among mortals. And this points to a very mysterious context.

We must now sketch in a few words, and bring before your souls, the nature of temple sleep, which was one of the remedies employed by the priests of Egypt. Anyone who had suffered loss of health in any way in those days was not as a rule treated with external remedies; there were only few of these, and they were seldom used. Sufferers were in most cases taken to the temple and there put into a kind of sleep. It was not an ordinary sleep, but a kind of somnambulistic sleep[7] which was intensified so that the patient became capable not of chaotic dreams merely, but of seeing real visions. During this sleep the patient perceived etheric forms in the spiritual world, and the wise priests understood the art of influencing these etheric pictures which passed before the sleeper, of controlling and guiding them.

Let us suppose that a patient was put into a temple sleep. The priest skilled in medicine was at his side when he fell into this somnambulistic sleep. The patient then entered a world of etheric forms, and the priest, because of the power he possessed through his initiation (only possible in those ancient times when conditions of life were ones that no longer or very seldom exist today), was able to control the entire course of the patient's sleep. He formed and fashioned the etheric visions and entities such that there actually appeared before the sleeper, as if by magic, those forms which at one time the ancient Atlanteans had looked on as their gods. These divine forms—concerning which the various peoples still possessed a memory, in the German, Norse and Greek mythologies—were now placed before the soul of the person in the temple sleep. He saw, in particular, certain figures which were connected with the healing principle.

Had the patient remained conscious, as in the waking consciousness of today, it would not have been possible for such forces to act upon him; this was only possible in somnambulistic sleep. The wise priest guided this dream-life in such a way that powerful forces were liberated during the etheric visions, and these restored to order and harmony the forces of the body which had fallen into disorder and discord. This was only possible when the waking consciousness of the patient had been suppressed. Temple sleep had therefore a very real significance, and we can see how the healing art of the priests was connected with knowledge only accessible to the human being through initiation. The connection lies clearly before us. It was the priests who, through the revival of the ancient vision of higher worlds, possessed in their wisdom the forces which came from these worlds, enabling spirit to work upon spirit. They acquired the capacity of allowing spirit to work upon spirit, and by this means wisdom was brought into inner connection with health.

In the uplifting of the self to what was spiritual there was, in ancient times, a healing element, and it would be well if people were to learn to understand this again, for they would then understand the great mission of the anthroposophic movement, which is to lead human beings up to the spiritual world, so that they may again enter those worlds from which they have descended. It is true that in future people will not be put into a somnambulistic condition; self-awareness will be fully maintained; yet strong spiritual forces will nevertheless become active in them, and the possession of wisdom and insight into higher worlds will then be capable of acting on human nature to harmonize and heal. Today this connection between spirituality and the healing art is hidden, and those who are not initiated into the deeper wisdom of the mysteries cannot discern the connection, or even observe the subtler realities they encounter. Those who look more deeply know upon what profound inner conditions a case of healing may depend. Let us suppose for example that a certain illness befalls someone and that it has an inner cause—not a fractured thigh–bone or a stomach upset, for these are external causes. Anyone wishing to study this deeply will very soon find that someone who is greatly preoccupied with mathematical ideas will have a state of health very different from those who do not occupy themselves with such things. This fact indicates the remarkable connection between a person's mental life and the state of their outward health. It is not, of course, as if mathematical thinking healed someone. Let us look at this more closely: we find that those who apply themselves to mathematics have need of healing in a way that is different from those who do not. Suppose two people have exactly the same illness—in reality this never happens, but we may suppose it. One of them does not care to know anything about mathematical ideas; the other is intensely interested in them. It might be quite impossible to cure the non-mathematical person whereas the other could possibly be cured with suitable remedies. What I have stated is an actual fact.

Take another example. We have two people before us: one is an atheist in the crassest sense, the other a deeply religious person. Again it might happen that if both have the same disease and the same remedy is used that the religious person can be cured and the other not. These are things which to modern thinking—at least to the greater part of humanity—will seem absurd; however, they are not. How is this? It depends on the fact that an entirely different influence is exercised upon human nature by so-called 'sense-free' ideas than by ideas governed entirely by sense perceptions. Think for a moment of the difference between a person who likes mathematics and one who does not. The latter says: 'I ought to think about these things—but I only want to think of things which I can perceive with my senses!' Yet it is of great value to our inner being to dwell on conceptions of what cannot be seen. Hence it is useful to have religious conceptions, for these also relate to things which cannot be grasped with the hands, nor have any connection with outer, material things—in a word with things which are sense-free. These are matters which one day, when people become more preoccupied with the spiritual, will have a great influence on educational principles. For example, let us take the simple conception 3 x 3 = 9. Children form such a conception best when they do it without the help of anything material. It is not good when they put 3 x 3 beans next to each other for too long, for then they do not rise at all above the sense world; but if you accustom children, to begin with, not for too long, to count on their fingers, and then follow it with pure mathematical thinking, such thought has a curative, harmonizing effect upon the children. How little people of the present day understand such things can be seen from the fact that in their system of instruction the exact opposite occurs. The abacus has been introduced into our schools, using different coloured beads to make addition, subtraction, etc., apparent to sensory eyes. In this way what ought to be comprehended purely in the mind is said 'to be made tangible' to the senses. It may be convenient, but those who consider this to be educational know nothing of that deeper curative education which is rooted in the power of the spirit. Someone who, from childhood on, has been accustomed to live with sensory thoughts will have a nervous system that has lived under sickly conditions, and it will be harder to cure them than to cure someone who has been accustomed to sense-free ideas from an early stage. The more people are accustomed to think independently of sensory objects, the easier it is to cure them.

In ancient times when anyone was ill it was customary to place before them all kinds of symbolic figures, triangles, and combinations of numbers. The aim, besides the other value these things possessed, was to uplift them from mere outward vision of things. If I place a triangle before me and merely look at it, that has no particular value but if on the other hand I see it as the symbol of the higher triad of the human being it becomes a healing conception in the mind. Observe how the conceptions of spiritual science lead us to the vision of spiritual things. We are led from what takes place on earth to what has taken place on Old Sun, Moon, and Saturn. With physical eyes we cannot see the events of those times, nor can we reach up to Old Moon or Old Sun with sensory hands. Yet without the aid of the external crutches of our senses we can uplift ourselves to the things which existed once upon a time; we can acquire conceptions which have an equalizing and harmonizing effect upon our whole life and likewise upon our body. Spiritual science will again prove to be a great, a universal remedy, as it was formerly in the hands of the Egyptian priests; at that time, however, it required suppression of the I, as in temple sleep.

The spiritual conception of the world is a curative conception. Many people will say in answer to this assertion: Are all anthroposophists healthy people? Do none of them fall ill? We must understand that fundamentally the individual can do very little for their health and sickness. The causes of disease lie outside the individual personality in a large proportion of cases. Someone may have the healthiest ideas, which, if they were to live under quite healthy conditions, would result in their never suffering internal illness; but today there are other causes beyond the control of the individual: the secret causes of heredity for example, the influences passing from one human being to another, the influences of an unnatural environment, etc. All these influences, which are external, hidden, causes of disease, can only gradually be alleviated by a healthy anthroposophic outlook. Although we may observe that a person who is inwardly most healthy may fall ill, even dangerously ill, we must not regard this as a sign that spiritual science will fail to act curatively upon humanity in the course of centuries—I say centuries, not thousands of years. Before spiritual vision a vista unfolds of a future when no inner cause of sickness will exist for those able to engender the inner and outer conditions of spiritual wisdom. But external causes there will always be, and these can only be eradicated as a spiritual-scientific art of healing gains more and more ground.

When we rightly understand the effect of what is spiritual we find that temple sleep is not unintelligible to us. What was conjured up in the etheric visions of the sleeper in the temple? It was the picture of the Atlantean gods whom we once knew as etheric forms; among whom we once lived, when we were able to be conscious outside the physical body and could exercise etheric clairvoyance. If we go still farther back in human evolution, far beyond the Atlantean epoch, we reach a period in which human beings first became what they now are, when they first appeared as the individual personalities they are today. This period is called the Lemurian epoch. The Atlantean continent, from which the people spread to Africa, Europe, and Asia, came to an end through catastrophic inundations. Lemuria, on the other hand, which was that portion of the earth upon which humanity dwelt before the Atlantean epoch, was destroyed by the forces of fire, by volcanic catastrophes. It was during the Lemurian epoch that the human being first gained consciousness of the I, a mighty impulse in human evolution. How did the human being attain 'I' or ego consciousness?

It is very difficult for materialistic thought of today to conceive of this ancient condition of humanity. Were you to imagine the human being of that time as similar to the human being of today, with flesh and blood, bones and muscles, your idea would be entirely wrong.

At that time the human being possessed a far more impermanent, a far softer form; the human body was comparatively fluid. What later became muscles and bones has only grown hard in the course of time. At that period also human reproduction was entirely different. The human being lived more in the earth's atmosphere, which at that time was not pure air as it is today, but was filled with all kinds of vapours. In this the human being lived as an actual form of air, and the currents surrounding the earth passed in and out of him. The human form was almost the same as some cloud we see today which continually changes its form, except that the form of the human being at that time was somewhat firmer and more defined. There appeared then, also for the first time, what are now described as the sexes; at that period of evolution an ancient, non-sexual kind of propagation was replaced by a sexual one. This took place, however, millions and millions of years ago.

Simultaneously with sexual reproduction came the embodiment of the earliest germ of the I. Previous to this human beings were impelled to reproduce their like through external influences which lay in spheres surrounding them. That was the form of reproduction at a time when human beings did not yet possess an I, when they still had a dim clairvoyant consciousness, when they rested entirely in the 'bosom of the godhead' and could not say, 'I am'. Their form of perception was somewhat as follows: they were aware that when they did anything it made an impression upon their spiritual environment, and they felt their existence to partake of this environment. Rather than being able to say: 'I am here', they felt something like 'My environment allows me to be here.' They lay within the bosom of the living earth, and the living forces of the earth streamed out of and in to them. At that time there were no unhealthy forces; disease did not exist; there was no death such as we know it. It was only when, with sexual reproduction, the human being became endowed with an I, that sickness and death entered. Before that human beings were not conceived by their like but, in the same way that we breathe nowadays, they absorbed substances from their environment, and in this environment lay the fertilizing forces that entered them, and caused them to bring forth their kind.

These forces within human beings and their offspring were healthy, health-giving. The priests of Ancient Egypt knew this, and they said: The further we guide a person's vision back to previous conditions the more do we return him to conditions in which there is no disease. Vision of the old Atlantean gods acted curatively, and this was still more true when the priests guided these visions so that the temple sleeper saw before him those primeval forms which were fertilized not from their like but from what lived in their environment. The sick person who lay in the temple sleep beheld the form of the one who bore her kind without receiving fertilization from her kind: the generating woman, the virginal woman with child, the goddess who in the Lemurian epoch was the companion of humankind and who has since disappeared from human vision. In Ancient Egypt she was called the sacred Isis.

Isis could only be seen as a matter of course by humankind when death had not yet appeared on earth. At that time human beings, in their normal consciousness, were the companions of such figures who floated around them, and brought forth their kind virginally. When Isis was no longer the visible companion of humanity, when she had withdrawn into the circle of the gods, she continued—as the priests said—to interest herself in the health of the human being from the spiritual world. And when someone was raised to vision of those ancient forms, to that image of the sacred Isis, in a way that was out of the ordinary, as in temple sleep, the goddess still brought healing to him. She is that principle in the human being which existed in us before we received our mortal sheath. Her veil no mortal has raised, for she is the form which existed before death had entered the world. She is rooted in the eternal, the great healing principle to which humanity will again attain when it steeps itself anew in spiritual wisdom. We see what has remained of this in the wonderful symbol of the Madonna and Child. Speaking from the standpoint of spiritual science we can emphatically say that we see it in many pictures of the Madonna. We can state that these pictures have a curative effect; for, within the limits which have been discussed, a picture of the Madonna is a means of healing. When it is viewed and studied in such a way that it has an after-effect upon the human soul, when this human soul can dream during sleep about the Madonna picture, it then possesses a healing power even today.

Let us now ask about the nature of the fertilizing forces at a time when human beings were not yet fertilized by their own kind. Think of our earth at that time as being a solid kernel surrounded by all kinds of viscous, seething substances, mingled with vapour, and in this half-watery structure dwelt Lemurian humanity. The sun, which could not then be perceived by human eyes, because our sense organs had not developed, shone down upon the earth; the sun's influence, however, penetrated through the veils of mist and cloud, and with the power of the sun's rays the earth also received fertilizing powers. The earth did not only receive the forces of warmth, but at the same time the forces which today live in the power of fertilization. What the human being absorbed streamed to the earth from invisible, spiritual sun beings. Such was the relationship between sun and earth. The power which acted at that time upon those genderless, self-propagating human forms, was perceived as a masculine power. This sun effusion was poured out over the whole earth. Such were the conditions during the early part of the Lemurian epoch.

But let us now go back still further, to a period in which the conditions were again quite different, to a primeval past when the sun, which is now separate, was bound up with our earth. At one time the earth and the sun formed a single body. All that is finer and more etheric was still connected then in a sense within this common body. At this time the two were connected in a way that resembles a double biscuit, with one part, a smaller globe (namely the earth-plus-moon) appended to the other. We must imagine the sun as a vast etheric body to which the earth-plus-moon was appended. The rays of energy from the sun still mingled with the earth, passing from the sun to the earth and back again from earth to sun—for the two were in a certain way united.

We shall best understand the purpose of this process of evolution if we ask what would have happened if, without anything further taking place, the sun had turned entirely away from the earth after separating from it, and had no longer sent its beams and rays to the earth? All life upon the earth would in this case have desiccated and hardened. It was necessary for the earth that the sun's fertilizing influences should remain. We have to regard this interplay between sun and earth as the interplay between two principles: one leading to densification and rigidity, the other engendering continual life. This was also the case later: invigorating life flowed continually from the sun to the earth.

We have now briefly recapitulated the various stages in the evolution of our earth. First there was a primeval past when the earth was still within the sun-body; then a second stage in which the earth was more loosely connected with the sun; then a third, when the two bodies were completely separated from each other. It was only in this third epoch that the I really entered the human being, and at this stage sexual reproduction began. Then followed the fourth epoch, the Atlantean, and lastly the post-Atlantean epoch, in which we are now living. To those who look more deeply into the fabric of the world, all that happens visibly, all that is external, takes place under the influence of spiritual beings. At one time the sun and the earth were one. (We will consider the moon's role later.) This common body was then permeated with harmoniously working divine spiritual beings. Such lofty beings were necessary to govern forces which at that time were still bound up together.

Now think of a somewhat further stage of evolution: the sun withdrew. What took place then? With the sun went forth the highest beings and the finest substances; henceforward they worked upon the earth from outside. Beings who embodied truly living, ever-sustaining life, dwelt upon the sun; and on the earth the beings who, if they had been left to themselves, would have suffered stiffening, rigidity, darkness. At this second stage of evolution light and darkness were both at work.

At the third stage of evolution the human being is endowed with the I, and the time begins when this self-aware 'I' dwells within him. He becomes aware of this I especially through its opposite, and he gradually passes into one condition in which he has a clear consciousness, and into another in which he has a dim consciousness; the first comes to him from the sun, and the other primarily from the earth. The I, the eternal seed, has to alternate between two forms, one an eternal form, and the other a form which can be born and can die. Those beings, who always possess what the human being has only occasionally, depart from the earth. First that being who brings about fertilization departs to live principally on the sun, then the being who preserves the duration of the human form departs with the moon.

Sun and moon gradually separated from the earth. With the sun departed the beings who, had they remained united with it, would have brought too burgeoning a life to earth; and with the moon all those forces withdrew which would have brought about a hardening and stiffening; everything which would have tended to make form permanent. The earth remained in the midst, as it were between the two. The human being on earth alternates between these two, is influenced on the one hand by the sun, and on the other by the forces of the moon. Thus beings who were previously the human being's companions had now withdrawn, some to the sun and some to the moon.

In the fourth epoch of the earth's evolution we find those companions of the human being who had condensed to the level of an etheric-divine body, and who in certain respects were subject to human weaknesses. These were the etheric gods with whom humankind lived during the Atlantean period. In post-Atlantean times humanity lost its connection with these etheric gods also, entering entirely into the physical world so that the door to spiritual worlds was shut. There remained to us, however, from these ancient times, something like a memory of spiritual worlds, and in accordance with the law of recapitulation, everything we had passed through in life at one time woke up within us later as knowledge. We had lived through numerous epochs in which we were variously related to the gods. We now passed through the same stages again, but with knowledge.

After the great Atlantean flood, in the first era of civilization of Ancient India, the human being once again experienced in soul and spirit that epoch when earth and sun had been united. The very exalted deity who guided and governed everything that the human being experienced in the first post-Atlantean civilization was called by a name back then which was preserved as tradition in later eras: Brahman, the All-One. This deity actually dwelt among humankind at one time. In the first epoch of the evolution of our earth, the human being was the companion of Brahman—who was revered in ancient Indian civilization and was perceived by the people of those times in an elevated state.

Then followed the Persian civilization during which mankind consciously experienced the second epoch of evolution, when the sun with its all-invigorating forces had separated from the powers of darkness. For this reason people perceived a duality in the godhead in the second cultural epoch, and this duality is represented as the opposition of Ormuzd, the good deity, and Ahriman, the destroying deity. This was nothing but a repetition—but in knowledge—of what the human being had actually experienced in earlier ages.

We then come to the memory of the epoch when the sun and moon had departed from the previously united celestial body, the sun with its fertilizing forces and the moon with forces which gave form: to the human being a transitory form, and to the gods a permanent one. In the Egyptian age this difference was perceived in the opposition of earlier forces to those still at work, but now their opposition was of a different kind. In Egypt the solar forces were perceived as the forces of Osiris. Osiris was the power of the sun as it worked in the third epoch of earthly evolution, and the religion of Osiris arose and flourished in this age. Isis represents the power of the moon before its complete separation from the earth, before the division of the sexes, when the virginal power of reproduction was still operative. Later Isis fled to the moon, where she became rigidified.

In the fourth age, that of Greco-Roman civilization, humanity experienced in polytheism a memory of the Atlantean epoch with its numerous figures of the etheric gods.

And now in our cultural epoch, the fifth, we have nothing to re-experience. Let us bring this thought before our minds: we have nothing to repeat, no ancient memories. We have given birth to a fifth age of civilization, one whose results will be seen in the future, while the four previous ages were repetitions of the four preceding cosmic epochs. Our age must give birth not merely to an ancient wisdom, but to a new wisdom, a wisdom which points not only to the past, but which must work prophetically—apocalyptically—into the future. In the mysteries of past ages of civilization we see an ancient wisdom preserved, but our wisdom must be an apocalyptic wisdom, the seed for which must be sown by us. Once again we have need of a principle of initiation so that the primeval connection with spiritual worlds may be renewed.

The task of the anthroposophic movement is to supply this principle. No wonder that wisdom has been lost to so many, for without the principle of initiation it is very difficult nowadays to obtain wisdom, more difficult than formerly when the memory of ancient experiences had only to be refreshed, and when the consequences of earlier stages of evolution could be made conscious to humankind. Today this is difficult; therefore we can understand that the sense-world seems to be devoid of God, to be barren and empty; but although it appears as if the ancient spirit-world had died out, it is there. It is active and fruitful and if human beings so will, they can find connection with the spiritual world.

Care was taken, precisely at the moment when the ancient memories seemed to be disappearing during the Greco-Roman age, that a wonderful new seed for all future time should be laid within the cold ground of the earth; this seed is what we call the Christ principle. The apocalyptic wisdom, the true new spiritual wisdom, will be found in conjunction with this Christ principle, which does not point back only to memories of past epochs, but prophetically to the future, and precisely through this it summons the human being to action, to creative work. This productive wisdom has sprung freely from seed that was sown in the past. So we see a far horizon of the future rise before us when we speak of the universe, the earth and the human being. In what follows we shall have to speak not merely of the past, but also of the forces of the future. The world is not merely concerned with what is past, it evolves towards the future, and our earth still has a long period to pass through before it ends. The human being's futurity, however, extends beyond the earth, and if we are to know ourselves completely, the full scope of our human nature, we must look not to the past alone but must study what is at work today and what will go on working into the world's great tomorrow.

LECTURE 3

STUTTGART, 6 AUGUST 1908

The Kingdoms of Nature and Spirit Beings

IF we are to bring the relationships between universe, earth, and human being before our minds in the following lectures, it will first be necessary to gather together many things that will furnish us with some kind of foundation. At the same time we must remember that if we only use our external senses and the intellect bound up with these, we shall survey very little; this applies to the earth as well as to the human being, and in a still greater degree to the universe. We must realize that the greater part of what is most essential is hidden from the outer senses, and also from external intellectual observation. Therefore to begin with we will point out a few things related to the beings that surround us but which are hidden from view. Much will have to be said which many of you know already, but in order to grasp our vast subject thoroughly it will be necessary to recapitulate to a certain extent. We must in the first place consider the planet on which we live, which forms the centre of our studies.

Yesterday we considered one portion of the earth's evolution in connection with the whole. We saw how beings have been active in various ways, from the time when earth and sun still formed one body up to our own day. We saw also that in the various ages of the post-Atlantean epoch, the human being has recapitulated in knowledge and in religious consciousness all that the earth has passed through in the course of its evolution.

We will now look more deeply at the various conditions on this our earth. We are surrounded in the first place by the four kingdoms of nature; the mineral, plant, animal and human kingdoms. The human being is not the merely material, physical being of which the outer senses inform us, and which the scientific intellect describes and explains, but a complex entity composed of physical body, etheric body, astral body and I. All this we know. When we allow our gaze to sweep over the beings of the other kingdoms of the earth we must be fully aware that the expressions physical body, etheric body, astral body and I also certainly relate to them also. When dealing with the physical world we have to allow that of all earthly beings the human being alone possesses an ego- or I-nature; we alone in this physical world have a self-aware I. With animals it is quite different; the I of animals is not in the physical world in the same way that the human I is.

If we consider the difference between animals and human beings we must acknowledge that whereas each of us human beings has an individual 'I' enclosed as a single individuality within our skin, not every animal has an I. Rather, particular groups of similarly formed animals have one I or ego in common. For example, all lions, or all bears, have a common I, hence we call such an I belonging to the animal kingdom a group ego. The human I is found in the physical world; although we may not see it with our eyes it is present within the skin of every human being. This is not the case with animals. We do not find their group ego in the physical world. In order that you may form an idea of such a group ego imagine that there is a partition before me, and in this partition ten holes. I put my ten fingers through the holes and move them. You see my fingers but not myself, and without much deep thought you say that these ten fingers do not move by themselves, but something hidden must be causing the movement; in other words you think of a being that belongs to the fingers. This comparison brings us to the group-nature or soul-nature in the case of animals.

The various lions on the physical plane are beings which, in a certain sense, have also something hidden behind them. Just as the central being belonging to the ten fingers is hidden by the partition, so something is also hidden which is common to all lions. It is hidden because it is not present at all in the physical world. The same I-nature which in the case of the human being is present in the physical world is to be found, in animals, in the astral world. The group ego of animals is in the astral world. From each single animal there stretches a sort of extension of its being into the astral world: there these extensions combine and form the garment or sheath of the animal-I. These group egos live as single individuals on the astral plane, just as human individual egos or 'I's do here on the physical plane. When we enter the astral plane clairvoyantly, we encounter the various animal egos as separate beings which extend their principles into the physical world. One must not merely picture this diagrammatically, but must accustom oneself to picture these egos in their reality. It must be clearly understood that we do not have to go into another region to enter the astral world; the astral world permeates our physical world. It is only a case of our being able to look into it with opened astral perceptions.

You may now ask what the group egos of animals look like. The group ego of one of the higher orders of animals appears to the clairvoyant somewhat as follows: along the spine of the animal is seen what resembles a brightly shining line. As a matter of fact our atmosphere is permeated not only by the material currents generally recognized, but also in every direction by astral currents, and in these currents the clairvoyant recognizes the group egos of animals.

A second question might now be asked: Have lower beings, such as plants for example, an I or ego too? Yes, they do. On examining a plant with clairvoyant perception we find that the aspect visible in the physical world is nothing but a combination of the physical and etheric bodies of the plant. Imagine the surface of the earth on which plants grow, picture the root of a plant, the stem, the leaves, and flowers. Unlike the human being, what grows in the physical world as a plant does not have an astral body and I, but only a physical and etheric body. We must not conclude from this that the astrality with which we are filled, and which is active also in animals, is not active in the plant. To the opened eyes of the clairvoyant the plant is surrounded by a glow, and this comes from astral substances. It is this also which cooperates in the development of the flower. While the plant grows from leaf to leaf through the influence of the etheric body, its growth terminates above in a flower through the effect of the surrounding astral substance. The clairvoyant sees every growing plant thus surrounded by astral substance, but there is something else connected with the plant, namely its I or ego. If we wish to locate the I of a plant we must seek it in the centre of the earth. There the I of all plants is to be found; this is an important and essential truth. Whereas we see the I of animals in the circumference of the earth, we must turn to the centre of the earth for the I of plants. In fact, when clairvoyant vision has attained to such a view of the plant cover of the earth, which people otherwise perceive only as a material entity, it enlarges into an organism with an I at its centre, an I that consists of all plant 'I's together.

The earth is ensouled by an ego or I and in the same way as your head is covered with hairs which grow forth from your being, so plants grow forth from the being of the earth and belong to the whole organism of the earth. When one tears a plant up by the roots it hurts the whole earth, the soul of the plant experiences pain. This is a fact. On the other hand one should not think that the earth feels pain when a flower is plucked; exactly the reverse is the case. For example, when in autumn a reaper cuts corn the clairvoyant sees great currents of a sense of well-being pass over the earth. Objections to this from the moral standpoint do not hold good. You might think perhaps that a child plucking all sorts of plants uselessly should cause more pain than someone, with good intention, carefully transplanting. Yet the fact remains that the earth feels pain if a plant is uprooted but feels pleasure when it is plucked. You see, the earth takes pleasure in yielding up what it bears on its surface. Likewise when animals graze upon plants the earth has a sensation of pleasure, much the same as a cow has when her calf draws milk. This is an absolutely true esoteric fact. The sensation of the earth when plants spring from it and are shone upon by the astral body is the same as that of animals when they yield their milk. These are not merely comparisons, but are actual facts. Anyone who can see into the astral world with clairvoyant vision still sees nothing of the I of plants; to do this a higher clairvoyance is required, by which it is possible to see into the devachanic world. We can say, therefore, that the group ego of animals is in the astral world, whereas the ego of plants is in the devachanic world.

The next question that naturally presents itself concerns the mineral world. How is it with so-called lifeless minerals? Have they anything resembling an ego, or some other higher principle? If we observe a stone clairvoyantly we find that in the physical world it has only a physical body; but the etheric body of minerals surrounds and envelops this on all sides. Take, for example, a rock crystal; you must imagine this entire form as hollowed out, resembling a hollow space, and only where the physical substance ends does the etheric begin. Just as the upper part of a plant is surrounded by the astral, so the etheric realm surrounds the mineral. This etheric is at home in the astral world. Please note this particularly: here we have an etheric that is at home in the astral world. Things are really more complex than is generally supposed. It is not the case that in the astral world everything is astral; this is as little the case as that in the physical world everything is physical. For example, in the physical world you have the etheric body, the astral body, and even the human I; and the clairvoyant also sees the etheric body of minerals in the astral world.

Now let us ask where the astral body of minerals dwells. This looks like rays with a distinctive form. Picture to yourselves forms of light, or rays that broaden ever wider, and pierce the etheric body of the mineral. Astral rays stream thus from every mineral. They have no end, but stream out infinitely into space. When observing a rock crystal you see first the space which is physically occupied; clairvoyantly you see this physical form surrounded by the light of the etheric body, and this again as if pierced by all kinds of rays which extend endlessly in all directions into space. Vision is led from each point of space that is filled by some substance into the infinite. There is no point of space that is not connected with the universe: it is as if every single thing in the world hung on thousands and thousands of threads of spiritual light which stretch into infinite space, and you can imagine that if these extended ever further, they would all ultimately converge.

In fact, when a mineral is studied clairvoyantly, something like the following appears: the physical part is seen as surrounded by the light-forms of the etheric body; then rays of light appear to broaden and radiate continually into space till they ultimately disappear as if into a hollow globe. You can think of every mineral as being the centre of such a hollow globe, and that these are present everywhere in the world. These hollow globes interpenetrate each other, and if we can picture clairvoyant power enhanced more and more to where these rays unite, we arrive at where the egos of the minerals stream towards us from every direction of space. These egos reveal themselves to clairvoyant perception when it enters the higher regions of the devachanic plane. Whereas the rays which compose the astral body dwell in the lower regions, these egos exist in the higher devachanic world.

Here therefore we have a survey of the different kingdoms. The I of the human being is on the physical plane, that of animals on the astral plane, that of plants in the lower regions of the devachanic world, and the I of minerals is in the higher regions of the same world. The minerals on earth are therefore in a sense in a situation that is the reverse of ours. We have an I within us, enclosed within our skin; each of us is a centre in ourselves, a 'human centre'. Plants form a wider centre; taken together they form an 'earth centre'; and the egos of minerals form the encompassing periphery of the cosmos. Wherever the human being is found the human I is always the centre; the mineral I is always in the periphery or circumference—exactly the opposite of the human being. You will now find it comprehensible when I tell you that the mineral soul is in an entirely different position from that of the human or the animal soul.

When a mineral is broken up it does not feel pain, on the contrary it feels pleasure, it has a sensation of well-being. Great currents of pleasurable feeling stream forth from a quarry where stones are broken to pieces; on the other hand were you to assemble all the broken pieces together again it would cause very great pain. The same fact may be observed in another process. Imagine that you have a glass of warm water into which you throw a piece of salt. When the salt dissolves not only does the substance dissolve, but feelings of well-being fill the warm water, feelings of pleasure on the part of the mineral at being dissolved. Again, if you cool the water so that the salt crystallizes, the process is connected with a feeling of pain. Initiates have always known these things and have described them; one must only learn to understand what they say. One of the greatest initiates spoke about this.

Let us picture how things were at one time in the earth's evolution. Today we walk on solid earth, but it was not always thus. When we trace the evolution of the earth backwards we find that it becomes ever softer and softer till at last its condition is fluid or even vaporous. What is solid today, namely the mineral part, has crystallized out of the once fluid earth. It had to become solid so that human beings might walk upon it. It was necessary for human existence that the earth, in its mineral nature, should suffer infinite pain—for infinite pain was connected with the solidification of the earth. Paul said, referring to this: 'For we know that the whole of Creation travails and groans in pain',[8] meaning that the earth has to endure birth-pangs in connection with solidification, and formation of the mineral earth so that God may at last receive us human beings as his offspring.

We need never lose respect for the writings of true initiates when we come to understand them; every line of the inspired biblical record fills us with profound awe when we learn its meaning with the help of spiritual science. Cosmic secrets are hidden in the saying of Paul quoted above. It is true that such truths as these will only again become fruitful for humanity when they enter into and affect our feelings. They must not be only comprehended intellectually, but must be embodied in feeling if they are to become true knowledge.

Let us now once again consider plants—how their physical body grows, how the glow of the astral body surrounds this, and how their I is at the centre of the earth. Let me point out once more what is essential in this. What does the astral body really do when it encompasses the flower from outside? It does something of great importance in the life of the plant, and we will understand this if we enter a little more deeply into the spiritual configuration of our earth. In the last lecture we learnt that there was a time when the earth and the sun formed one body. Human beings were already present though living under entirely different conditions from those of today. They possessed a dim clairvoyant consciousness; and their organism was such that they could dwell within that earth-sun body. Today our organization is such that when a sunbeam falls on our eye we 'see', that is, we see the sunbeam which penetrates to us from without, and we see by means of this sunbeam. This was not the case at the time when human beings were still one with the earth, within the sun. Then they saw the sunbeams from within; they saw the soul forces which permeated the sunbeams. What were these soul-forces? The forces permeating the sunbeams are the same as the forces within our astral bodies. Physical light is but the external body of the astral light which radiates from the sun, and the astrality gleaming around the upper part of the body of a plant is connected inwardly with the astral radiance from the sun. You have desires and impulses of will because you possess an astral body. In the case of plants it is desire, feeling and will that play round the blossoms. What plays around the plant seeks to absorb the soul of the sunbeam, and with the soul its purest part—the I; and it is this purest part which passes through the plant to the centre of the earth. The activity of the plant's I is expressed in the activity of the spiritual content of the sunbeam which passes through it to the centre of the earth. Thus earth, plant and sun work together. The spiritual powers of the sun are in fact continually being administered to the earth. And how? By means of the astral body playing round them; the blossoms, which long to absorb the soul of the sunlight, allow it to sink through their bodies into the earth. What is brought about outwardly in the physical world through the beams of the sun is but one side of its activity; the other acts in the plant at a soul level, as a longing for the soul of the light that streams to earth in the rays of the sun.

Let us now try to understand the practical outcome of these things. Imagine a human being in a far distant future who perceives in every plant what I have just told you of its longing to absorb the soul of the sun. This human being will have, at a higher spiritual stage, something that the animal has at a lower stage. When grazing in a meadow it chooses the plants that are of use to it and leaves others alone: an unconscious instinct, but really it is higher spirits who guide the animal. Future human beings will consciously approach plants that are of use to them, not as now when they reflect on which of them yield the best substances for their health; instead they will then have a vital relationship with every plant, knowing what each has absorbed, and what each can give them. Eating will not be for them a lowly occupation, but an act consummated with soul and spirit, for they will know that everything they eat is the outward form of something spiritual. In our intermediate, transitional age, when people know little about the vital inward relationship between themselves and the world, all kinds of surrogates have had to be created. Why have the initiates of all ages urged people to say grace before eating? The grace should be a token of the recognition that, together with the food, something spiritual enters into us.

We have seen how sensation and feeling alter when the human being acquires true wisdom. With a certainty as sure as the instinct of animals at a lower stage, human beings will know with shining clarity what they do; they will know because they will recognize the soul of what they absorb into themselves. Down to everyday details such as these we can trace the practical value of spiritual science for the future. Thus we can now consider the world with entirely different feelings, for we regard the earth not only as a body upon which the rays of the sun shine down, but as a living being which absorbs the soul of the sun through the astral mantle of plants; and we see the entire universe permeated by the mineral egos, we see how all these things are ensouled and filled with spirit.

We have now considered the four kingdoms of nature, the mineral, plant, animal and human kingdoms, but that is not the end of it. These are only the kingdoms which the normally evolved human being can see. We have already pointed out, however, that in the Atlantean epoch the human being was the companion of beings whose form at its most dense went no farther than an etheric body. Those figures which have remained as a memory in the legends of various peoples, the figures of Zeus, Apollo, etc., were actual to the ancient Atlanteans; they dwelt with them during sleep. Everywhere could be found beings who had not descended as far as corporeal embodiment.

Looking from the human being upwards to higher kingdoms, we have to begin with three kingdoms which interest us. In accordance with Christian esotericism, we call the kingdom immediately bordering on the human, the realm of the angels; they are also called spirits of twilight. Then there is a second kingdom, higher than the angels, the kingdom of the archangels; they are also called the spirits of fire. Lastly there is a still higher kingdom, that of the archai (original powers or primal beginnings), called also the spirits of personality. These are three kingdoms ascending above the human. I will try to tell you a little about the life of these kingdoms for they play a very positive part in our life. Just as we play a part in the life of plants when we till the ground, so these higher kingdoms influence the human kingdom. We shall best understand this if we consider the following: the human being has in the present epoch an I, an astral body, an etheric body and a physical body. How does further development come to pass? Through working continually upon ourselves. Today the human I is still in many respects powerless to affect the other principles of our being: we are still in many ways unable to control our passions, but are governed by them, that is, by our astral body. There is a great difference between human beings in this respect. Compare a cannibal who eats his fellow human beings with a high idealist such as Schiller[9] or Francis of Assisi.[10] You see here an advancing development which consists in us human beings increasingly learning to control our astral body through our I. A time will come when the I will do this completely, will entirely permeate and illumine the astral body. The human being will then have formed a higher principle, this principle we call manas or spirit self. This is nothing other than the astral body that has been transformed by the I.

When we observe the human being of today clairvoyantly we see that the astral body really consists of two parts: one that is already under the control of the I and one that we are not yet able to control. This latter is still filled with lower forces and impulses, and when the I drives these out, all kinds of powers accrue to the astral body. In order that the astral body should not be destroyed by the lower forces it must always be permeated and suffused by higher beings who control it in the same way that we ourselves will control it in the future when we have attained the goal of our evolution. The beings whose task it is to govern that part of the astral body which is still ungoverned by humankind are one stage higher than we are: they are the angels, or spirits of twilight. In fact one such spirit watches over every human being, and this spirit has power over the astral body; it is therefore no childish idea, but profound wisdom, to speak of guardian angels. These guardian angels have a great duty to perform.

Let us consider the course of a human life in its entirety. We know that it passes through many incarnations. At a given time—at a certain point in earthly evolution—the human being began to live as a soul, as an I, in his first incarnation on earth. He then died, there was an interval, then a new incarnation, and so it has gone on from incarnation to incarnation; and these will only come to an end at a far-off period of human evolution. We will then have passed through all our incarnations, and we will also have gained the power to govern our astral body perfectly. This cannot be done, at least not in the normal course of evolution, until we have passed through all our incarnations. Now an angel accompanies the inmost core of our being and guides us from incarnation to incarnation, so that we may truly fulfil our mission on earth. It is, in fact, as if we had been able, since the beginning of our lives on earth, to look up to an exalted spirit who was our prototype, one who could fully govern the astral body, and who said to us: 'When in future you pass beyond this earthly evolution you must have become like me.' It is the task of angels to guide the incarnations of human beings and, in a spiritual sense, it is exactly the same thing to say that we look up to our higher self, whom we must come to resemble more and more, or that we look up to our angel as our great exemplar.

As human beings work further upon themselves they will also transform the etheric body into buddhi, or life spirit; one day they will do this work consciously, but now already they are unconsciously working at this. Thus still higher spiritual beings also have to work today in all human etheric bodies—the task of the archangels or fire spirits. Now, human etheric bodies are not individually as different as human astral bodies. Every human being has their own particular virtues or vices, but in matters relating to the etheric body there is a certain similarity. This can be seen in the qualities peculiar to a race or nation. Because of this we see that each individual human being does not have an archangel connected with their etheric body, but that whole nations and races are guided by higher or lower spirits of fire. The peoples and races of the earth are indeed guided as a whole by archangels. Here our view expands to something which to many seems entirely abstract, but for those who are able to see into the spiritual world it is absolutely real. If anyone today speaks of the soul or spirit of a nation, this is considered an abstraction. It is not so for esoteric perception, which sees a whole nation as if embedded in a spiritual substance, which is the body of an archangel or fire spirit. From antiquity until now our evolution has been led and guided from people to people, from race to race, by the spirits of fire, whose bodies are the souls of nations and whose mission it is to guide the course of human evolution through the various races of the earth.

There is, however, something else which is independent of tribe, nation and race. In studying our present age we find much that is independent of such communities, yet manifests simultaneously in many. For example, if we look back to the twelfth century we see how certain similar spiritual tendencies occurred in all the peoples of Europe, above and beyond the spirit of the nation. A phrase has been coined for this, the 'spirit of the age'. This spirit of the age is a reality, and forms the body for still higher beings, called the spirits of personality, or archai.

From all that has been said you can see that our earth is embedded in a sphere of spirit, a spiritual atmosphere. From a mineral foundation this enables plants to spring forth, and animals and human beings walk on it; enveloping all this are exalted spiritual beings: those who guide individual human beings, those who guide whole communities of people and races, and then also other beings who guide the 'spirit of the age' or *zeitgeist* from one epoch to the next.

In this lecture we have tried to survey our earth, seeing also what it is in a spiritual sense, and the human being's connection with it all. At the same time a foundation has been laid on which we can usefully build what we have to say in subsequent lectures about the relationship between the universe, the earth and the human being.

Lecture 4

STUTTGART, 7 AUGUST 1908

The Outer Manifestations of Spiritual Beings in the Elements and Cosmic Stages of Evolution

In our last lecture we spoke of diverse spiritual beings who in a sense enlarge the various kingdoms of nature that surround us in the physical world. We learnt that minerals and plants have an ego or I as well as an astral body; and our spiritual view was extended to include a wealth of realities besides those that our physical eyes can see and that our physical intellect can comprehend. We learnt, further, that higher spiritual beings take part in human evolution on earth, and do so even at the level of single individuals.

Spiritual science sees each separate human being as in principle possessing dominion over their inner world, the world of their actions and will. But we know that the essential inner nature of the human being has passed through many incarnations, and that at the present stage of evolution human beings are normally incapable of extending their scope of action beyond a single incarnation. Higher powers must collaborate to give the necessary direction for working not only between birth and death, but also beyond death, from one incarnation to another. In Christian esotericism these spiritual beings are called angels, and in anthroposophic parlance spirits of twilight. In Rosicrucian esotericism they are also called the sons of life—all these designations will become clearer to you later. We also heard how human communities—races and peoples—are guided by an order of spirits called archangels, or fire spirits; and, lastly, how what goes beyond the confines of a community of people and finds expression in the 'spirit of the age', or *zeitgeist* is guided by the archai, also called spirits of personality or primal powers, or, in theosophic parlance, asuras. Spiritual beings are at work everywhere in the world, and thus we must realize that three more kingdoms have to be added to those immediately around us. We will now try to give some idea of the more external manifestations of these beings.

When we consider the earth from the ordinary physical standpoint we see it is made up of what we call earth, water, air and fire. These are the four primary conditions of external matter. What spiritual science names 'earth' is called 'solid'; everything fluid (not only water but quicksilver, for instance) is called 'water'; everything gaseous, 'air'; and everything that can be perceived as having any degree of warmth is thought of as permeated with a finer substance that we call 'warmth substance', the latter not an outward attribute but representing a continuation of the other states of matter. And thus we first identify the material world surrounding us.

Now the spiritual beings of whom we have spoken live in these various material elements, as if in external bodies. To anyone able to observe the world with clairvoyant vision what is known as the fluid element, especially water, is not only inhabited by the beings we know as aquatic creatures, such as fish, but, despite it being in permanent flux, despite no form living in it in fixity, it is inhabited by spiritual beings, actually embodied in it in continually changing forms although it is not possible to discern them with external vision. In this element live the beings whom we have described as angels, or spirits of twilight. Their physical body is in a form that is not embodied in any solid, clearly defined corporeality; and when old myths and legends tell of such water-beings it is no fantasy, but is entirely in accordance with reality.

Further, in what we know as the gaseous element, and particularly in our air, those beings live whom we called archangels. It is no fairy tale when in streaming currents of air, in the rushing storm, we see the bodily manifestation of this spiritual kingdom. (When I said that angelic beings dwelt in water it is primarily that form of water which permeates the air as watery vapour—fugitive and fleeting and dispersed in separate atoms, in which clairvoyant vision perceives angels embodied.) Then, in what we know as the element of warmth we have the embodiment of beings known as the spirits of personality or archai. And since we human beings are composed of these four elements, earth, water, air, and fire, we have mingled within us not only the four elements, but also the beings we have just named; they pervade our body in a sense, they pass in and out of our physical body just as material substances do.

The range of beings connected with us is not exhausted by those I have mentioned. Still higher beings have to do with the earth, the universe and humankind, beings who are at a higher stage even than the spirits of personality. There are beings, for example, who stream towards us in the light, which for us is a still finer condition than warmth. Wherever there is anything that sends forth light we recognize in this light the garment of exalted beings, those to whom Christian esotericism gives the name of exusiai, or powers, or spirits of form. It is they who give form to everything around us. Wherever things are seen with a distinct form this is due to the activity of these spirits.

We now see that what is active in the evolution of our earth as the spirits of succeeding ages, the time spirits, is controlled by the spirits of personality. The task of the spirits of form is still higher. We shall best understand what this is if we reflect that from the beginning of human evolution, that is, from the time of the first human incarnation, the time spirit has continually changed, that among the many spirits of personality different ones have governed succeeding ages. But beyond all that is accomplished by the time spirit something else is active which runs through the whole of earthly humanity. Since the mission of mankind first began on earth, spiritual beings have participated in working upon humanity, and it is they we have to thank for the fact that we can be active as human beings. As if from a higher kingdom, the spirits of form have ruled from the beginning of the earth over the spirits of personality manifesting, in the *zeitgeist* or time spirit, as archangels in diverse communities, and as angels for individual people; they principally guide and govern all these other spiritual beings. These spirits of form have the task of working on the earth as a whole: theirs is a planetary activity. Therefore when we go beyond the *zeitgeist* to the spirit of the whole of humanity we encounter the spirits of form.

Now you are aware that our earth, as a planet, is subject to the law of re-embodiment like the human being. Prior to its present embodiment our earth was what is called Old Moon. What we now regard as the mission of the earth did not then exist. The mission of Moon was different; each planetary condition has its own mission to fulfil within the mighty whole; nothing is merely repeated, everything is subject to the law of evolution. During that incarnation of the earth we call Old Moon, certain beings had a task similar to that of the spirits of form during Earth evolution, and in Christian esotericism these are called the spirits of motion, or virtues, or dynamis.

If we go back still further in evolution we arrive at a planetary condition of our earth which preceded that of Old Moon, the condition of Old Sun, which as you are aware has nothing to do with the sphere we now see in the heavens as the sun. A very exalted principle ruled upon Old Sun, in the same way that the spirits of form rule during Earth evolution, and the spirits of motion ruled during Old Moon. In Christian esotericism this principle is called the hierarchy of the spirits of wisdom, called also kyriotetes, or dominions. These beings governed during Sun evolution. Then we come to a still earlier planetary condition, that of Old Saturn, when the governing, directing beings were those we call the thrones, or spirits of will.

Thus we pass to greater and ever greater levels of spiritual beings, ones who do not merely govern changing conditions like the time spirit but who are concerned with the mission of planetary conditions that change only from one planetary embodiment to the next, such as the thrones, the spirits of motion, and the spirits of form. All these hierarchies are continually in some sort of connection with us, although not in such close, directly perceptible connection as the lower hierarchies. We will try to illustrate how these work into our earthly evolution, but in order to do this it will be necessary first to consider the evolution of the angels, archangels and archai.

These beings are all greater than the human being of today, but in the next incarnation of the Earth, which we call the Jupiter condition, humankind will be raised to the level at which the angels are now, and will continually expand to ever greater degrees of perfection. This is also the case as regards the evolution of the other beings; they were not always what they are now, they also have passed through lower stages of development. Take the angels for example. In earlier times these passed through their human stage as we are now doing on earth; this was on Old Moon, and it was because of the work they carried out upon themselves at that time that they have become the higher beings they are now. In the same way archangels passed through their human stage on Old Sun. At that time they were beings like us; today they have advanced two stages above us. The archai had their human stage upon Old Saturn. They were one stage higher than the beings who passed through their humanity stage on the Sun, and roughly three stages higher than the human being is today. But those beings whom we call the spirits of form, whom we look up to and rever as very exalted beings, passed through their human stage in a past that it is impossible for us to conceive of. When the embodiment of the earth first began, when the earth was Saturn, they had already advanced beyond their human stage of evolution.

What exaltation must fill our souls when we look up in thought to these beings! But even they are subject to the law of evolution, and although on Saturn they were greater than the humanity of today, they rose through ever higher and higher stages of development during the Sun and Moon periods, and on to the time of the Earth, till at last they have attained to such a degree of expansion and have so large a field of activity that they no longer have need of a planet in order to find there the substances through which they can exist.

Other beings have need of our earth in a certain way; the angels have need of water, the archangels of air, and the spirits of personality have need of fire; but the spirits of form no longer require our planetary conditions, hence it was necessary for them, when our earth began its development, to find another dwelling-place, and that was why they separated from it. It was no merely mechanical splitting asunder of matter, but heavenly bodies separated off from each other in order to provide a dwelling-place for spiritual beings. Spirits of form sundered from the earth its finer substances; in this way the sun originated and now sends its light down to the earth from without. In the sunlight the spiritual nature of the spirits of form streams down to us, hence I said that light is the garment of these spirits. When we see the bright light of the sun streaming down to us we see in it the garment of these spirits who send their guiding and directing forces to the earth from the sun, thus guiding the mission of the earth.

We have to think of Old Moon as a heavenly body similar to our earth, which toward its end passed through a spiritualizing process. What had been split asunder was reunited and converted into an undifferentiated condition. It then passed through a kind of cosmic sleep after which there emerged from the womb of the cosmos that nebulous etheric sphere which is the rebirth of Old Moon. For us this is no material mass, but within this globe dwell all those mighty beings whom we have named as the spirits of motion, of form, etc. Only the germ of the human being dwelt in this globe, as yet having no I; but all those spiritual beings who had passed through a certain degree of evolution were intimately connected with this nebula.

How does the materialistic hypothesis explain the emergence of the solar system from this nebulous mass? There is an experiment frequently done in schools to demonstrate how the solar system appeared. A small quantity of oil is placed in the middle of a heavier liquid and rotated by some simple mechanical device. It can then be observed how this globule becomes oblate, how drops break from it, how these form again into globes and circle round the larger globule; by this means we see, in miniature, how something resembling a planetary system originates through rotation. This acts most suggestively. Why should we not imagine that the same thing took place with the world? We can see demonstrated before us how, through rotation, the planetary system originates, we have it before our eyes. Only one thing is forgotten! Sometimes it is good to forget this one thing, but not in this case; here one has forgotten oneself! In this experiment, if there is no one there to rotate the axis, no planetary system can be produced. If one thought rightly and logically one would have to suppose a gigantic human being in cosmic space who set the axis in motion like a mighty spit! Now it is obvious that there is no giant in space; but something else is there, the nebula is not merely matter, it is inspired and permeated by the beings we have already mentioned who have certain needs and aspirations.

One kind of these beings animated one kind of matter, and others another, and it was these who, when a certain degree of maturity had been reached, undertook to bring about separation, so that the higher beings went forth with the sun, and those who had need of earthly materials and forces remained behind upon the earth. Within this seething primeval body all these spiritual beings were active and they gradually formed what today we know as our planetary system. There were some, for example, who had not quite attained the goal which was that of the spirits of form; they were backward in their development. These beings had progressed too far to make the earth their dwelling-place, but were not sufficiently mature to accompany the finer substances to the sun. There were two principal classes of these beings, and we shall later become acquainted with their effect upon the earth. For in the same way that the perfected and matured powers shone in sunlight upon the earth as spirits of form, guiding and governing it from the sun, so did these intermediate beings also direct the earth, but from a smaller compass as it were, which was, however, an exalted one compared with the human standpoint. It was in this way that Venus and Mercury originated between the sun and the earth; these are inhabited by beings at an intermediate stage. The other planets of our system have separated off in the same way through other beings having need of them as a field of activity.

Now let us again call to mind the time (during Earth evolution) when the sun departed with its beings, the earth remaining behind with all its potentialities, present humanity among them, who had not then reached their present stage. There were also other beings belonging to the animal and vegetable kingdoms that had already gone through a certain amount of evolution in the earth's previous embodiments, and these now reappeared in germinal form.

Let us to begin with consider the human being alone. Previous to this, when the sun was still one with the earth, mighty forces which proceeded from exalted sun beings were united with the earth, and worked upon the human being from within this planetary sphere. At first humankind was just as it had been on Old Moon, was only just evolving from this seed, as one might say, and was to begin with furnished only with a physical, etheric and astral body. The physical body was not so dense as it is now; it was more etheric and finer, and the I had not yet formed. Now, through the sun shining upon the earth from outside, and the sun-beings also working on it from without, conditions on earth changed completely. You can think of it in this way: as long as the earth was bound up with the sun, exalted beings (who later departed with it) were hampered in their own development, hence also in their powers, and power to govern—by the gross forces of the earth. But now that they had become free they could continue their evolution at a quite different rate from before, when they had to carry the very heavy weight of the earth mass with them. They freed themselves from the earth in their own evolution, and thus gained power to work on the human being more strongly from without.

Evolution would have been enormously accelerated through this, and human life would have been brought to an issue with extreme rapidity, if something else had not taken place. The human being was unable to proceed at this rate of development, therefore from the totality of previously existing spirits, one, with his hosts, separated from the rest, and remained united with the earth. The task of this spirit of form was to hold back and limit what the sun forces had accomplished with their enormous acceleration, so that these sun spirits did not work alone. If this spirit of form had remained connected with the earth and continued to work there, the whole earth would have grown rigid and hard, his influence would have been too powerful; therefore he took the grossest materials and forces away from the earth to constitute our present moon. So this spirit which had undertaken the duty of retarding and holding back the over-rapid development of humanity was now united with the moon.

Evolution continued once the earth-beings and the moon-beings had separated. Thus at this time the earth-beings came principally under the influence of two forces, one proceeding from the sun, the other from the moon. If the human being had merely been subject to the sway of the sun forces he would soon have grown old, almost as soon as he was born; whereas, under the influence of the moon alone he would have rigidified, become hard and mummified.

He could only develop rightly through the sun and the moon forces in balance: he was placed upon the earth and, in a spiritual sense, beings and forces acted on him from outside in order that he might pass through his present evolution.

We have seen how the human being is led from incarnation to incarnation by the beings we call angels; but these angels have no independence in the vast cosmos. They are governed by higher beings who dwell on the sun. Under the sole influence of these sun spirits all human development would have been compressed into one incarnation, whereas under the influence of the moon alone nothing at all would have taken place. Through the cooperation of these two sets of beings, the human being receives form from the moon forces, and receives from the sun what destroys form and leads the eternal part of us through our various incarnations. Thus if we consider things spiritually we see that everything in the world has its appointed task.

We shall now briefly consider in somewhat greater detail what took place at that time upon the earth. We know that when the human being emerged from Old Moon he possessed only his physical body, etheric body and astral body. At the time of the separation of the sun the physical body had not progressed far enough for the sense organs to be able to perceive external objects. These had certainly existed from the time of Saturn, but the human being could not use them to perceive external objects. Upon Old Moon the human being possessed organs which evoked pictures within him. The situation at that time was roughly as follows. Imagine one human being approaching another: he could not have perceived the other's external form, but a kind of dream picture would rise within him; and by the form and colour of the picture he knew that an enemy drew near, and that he must flee from him. This was picture consciousness, and had a real relationship to the soul qualities of the beings in one's vicinity.

Object consciousness only came to the human being gradually on earth. Though the sun as heavenly body was outside the earth, the human being could not at first see it, but perceived it only in pictures through an inner light. It is true that he did see in a certain sense, in a soul-spiritual way, the beneficial activities sent down to him by the spirits of the sun—he perceived these radiating in auric pictures, but they had nothing of the nature of our sense perceptions today. Thus there was a time when the sun forces sent their light to humankind, although in those times we could not see the external sun.

The separation of the moon from the earth took place somewhat later, and it was only at the stage of the moon's withdrawal that human beings were capable of acquiring the very first rudiments of I-consciousness, and only then began to feel themselves as separate beings; with this came also the power to perceive the first faint glimmer of physical objects. You can easily understand that sight is connected with I-consciousness, for as long as one cannot perceive an outer world one is not an I. Therefore the first flash of I-consciousness coincided with the first opening of human eyes to external objects. This was connected also with the moon's departure. Previously, when the moon was still united with the earth, it governed the forces of the individual's growth between birth and death—it does so still, but now from outside. But in order that the life of the human being should not be confined between birth and death, other forces had to approach humankind from outside; these were the sun forces. A continual interaction between the moon forces working from within, and the sun forces working from without, was associated with earthly development.

Try to picture vividly and exactly what happened next. So long as the sun was outside, but the moon still within the earth, human beings perceived the beneficial effect of the sun forces in inward pictures: they sensed the virtue of the sun forces, for these were always associated with the moon forces within the earth body, and had an effect upon the human constitution although remaining imperceptible. Then came the time when the moon also departed from the earth. Then the human senses were opened, and because of this humankind lost the power to perceive the soul and spirit aspect of the sun forces. Imagine the moment when spiritual perception disappeared and the first beginnings of actual sight with an outer view of the sun began, although in fact the human being could not yet see the sun, for the earth was shrouded in dense vapour. As opposed to the former dim clairvoyant perception, human beings were now able—if only gradually—to see the sun externally, although it was veiled by the density of the atmosphere. The beneficent effects of the sun were now withdrawn from human beings because of this advance in their development.

When the ancient Egyptian priests remembered this condition they gave the name of Osiris to the forces of the sun, those pure rays which human beings had perceived at one time through their dim clairvoyance. Humankind perceived Osiris no longer, and because of the vapours enveloping the earth, external perception of the sun was not yet possible; what the human being had previously seen was dead. 'Typhon the adversary had killed Osiris', the priests said, and those forces that had departed as moon, that were active between birth and death, now sought this ancient Osiris with longing.

Slowly and gradually the mist receded—it had endured for very, very long periods, even in the latter part of the Atlantean epoch; people now began to see the sun, but not as previously when all mankind had a common consciousness. The rays of the sun now fell on each individual eye when people gazed on the sun, and this was 'the dismembered Osiris'.

We are here concerned with a mighty cosmic event, and when we were incarnated as ancient Egyptians we recognized the recapitulation of this cosmic event. The wise Egyptian priests had this in mind, and describing it pictorially as follows, they said: 'At the time the moon and the sun departed from the earth, the human being remained in the middle, balanced between the solar and lunar forces.' Up to that time there had been no sexual reproduction, but only what might be called virginal reproduction. The forces which ruled our earth passed over from the sign of the Virgin, through the Scales, into the sign of the Scorpion. Therefore the priests of Egypt said: 'When the sun was in the sign of the Scorpion, and the earth in the Scales, his rays acted like a sting, stinging the sense organs to activity; thus Osiris was slain.' The emergence of external objectivity is the sting of the Scorpion, and came as something new, in marked contrast to the old virginal form of reproduction. It was then that humanity began its longing quest for its ancient power, for the vision of Osiris.

We must not look merely for astronomical facts in such a myth as that of Osiris, but we must see in it the result of the deep clairvoyant insight of the wise priests of Ancient Egypt. They embodied in this myth what they knew about the evolution of earth and human being.

Realities of the higher spiritual worlds lie at the foundation of all myths, and today we have shown how such realities form the foundation of the myth of Osiris.

Lecture 5

STUTTGART, 8 AUGUST 1908

Human Evolution in Relation to Cosmic Evolution

In previous lectures we have seen that the conditions of our earth have gradually evolved out of the cosmos; that in a far distant past the earth was one with the orb which shines in the heavens today as the sun, and that at a certain period this body separated off from the earth.

Now, I have stated that the beings who at first sent their own forces down from the sun to the earth, thus bringing about the evolution of humanity, are the spirits of form. These are the beings closest to earthly evolution. After the separation of the sun the leader of the spirits of form remained with the earth, and later departed from it with the moon. We can therefore speak of a moon-deity; he is called Jehovah in the Bible, and the sun powers, those who sent light to earth from without, are there called the Elohim, or spirits of light. Under the influence of the Elohim on one hand and Jehovah on the other, balance was maintained in human evolution. As we have seen, not only the human being evolves, but all the beings in the cosmos likewise do so. Those exalted beings who sent down their forces to us with the light—the spirits of form—have also undergone evolution; previously they were at a lower stage and have gradually worked their way upwards to their present position.

What was said just now about the Elohim and Jehovah applies to the most mature of these spirits, those who have made themselves fully capable of pursuing their development from the genesis of the earth onward, either upon the sun or the moon; but there are beings everywhere who have fallen behind at some stage. Yesterday we heard that planets such as Venus and Mercury owe their existence to the circumstance that beings at a level between the human being on the one hand and exalted sun spirits on the other, have remained behind. They required a dwelling-place more exalted than the earth, but were unable to inhabit the sun because they were not sufficiently mature. These beings are far beyond the evolution of humanity, but have not yet reached the condition of the sun spirits. They form a very important group of beings as regards human evolution. On one hand we have very mature beings, on the other, between them and mankind, are others whom we generally term luciferic beings, after their leader Lucifer.

Now we must try clearly to understand how Jehovah and the Elohim on the one hand, Lucifer and his hosts on the other, are concerned with human evolution. Through the cooperation of the sun gods with the moon god a duality arose, and we shall best understand what entered evolution at this point if we consider the nature of human evolution prior to that. Once more let us remind ourselves that the earth passed through a primordial incarnation, that of Saturn; then, after having passed through a state of rest, it entered upon Sun incarnation, then Moon incarnation, and lastly that of Earth. In the course of our evolution we have been connected with all these embodiments of the earth. As we know, we are a very complex being consisting of physical body, etheric body, astral body and ego, and these four principles play into each other in a very complex manner.

If any entity in our physical world had only a physical body it would be a stone—a mineral; in fact our mineral kingdom does only possess a physical body here on the earth. An entity possessing an etheric body in addition to a physical body possesses plant nature; our vegetable kingdom consists of such entities. An entity having physical, etheric and astral bodies is at the animal stage; and only a being who possesses an I in addition to these is at the stage of human existence on earth. Now it is only a rough way of speaking to say that as human beings we have these four principles within us; and we shall understand how schematic this is if we cast a glance back over our long, very long, evolution.

Which of these four principles is the oldest? It might easily be supposed that as the human I is the highest, making the human being human, it would be the oldest principle; but this is not the case.

Neither the I nor the astral body nor the etheric body was the first we possessed, but rather the physical body—it is the oldest. The first rudiments of the physical body were formed as far back as Old Saturn, but you must not imagine that this body looked then anything like the body of today. When you consider the present physical body you observe in the first place something solid, a skeleton, that firmly constituted part described as 'solid'; next you observe fluid constituents of many kinds; further, the physical body is permeated by the gaseous element, by air; lastly, you find in it something which, considered esoterically, is substantial—namely, warmth, inner warmth.

This inner warmth of ours does not depend upon our environment: in a cold environment we do not grow cold in the same way as minerals; we are not compelled to simply reflect our environment in this for we possess the source of our own warmth within us. Were you now to imagine away everything solid from the human being, also everything liquid and everything gaseous, and pictured our physical body formed only of warmth, such warmth as pulses in your blood, you will have what was present on Old Saturn. But that body did not have the form it does now: it had only the most rudimentary germs of a form. This was particularly the case in the middle of the Saturn period, for Saturn had initial, middle and late conditions. It would be very difficult to describe the early condition of Saturn, because few people have developed the capacity which would enable them to conceive of the conditions of Saturn before it became condensed to the consistency of warmth.

When in spirit you transport yourselves to that primordial past, you must not imagine that if you had been able to observe Saturn from somewhere in space you would have seen anything at all. Saturn had no light, it did not shine; only towards the end of its development did it begin to do so. Had you approached it in the middle of its evolution you would only have perceived its warmth, it was like an oven without external confines, yet self-limiting. You would have entered a field of warmth. You must not imagine this body of warmth as being uniform or homogeneous. If you had been sensitive to differences of warmth you would have found that there were currents of warmth within it in all directions, that they extended everywhere; you would have 'sensed' forms and regions of warmth. The whole of Saturn consisted of forms of warmth alone, and these were the original foundations of the human physical body. Saturn did go beyond this at the end of its development, though not in any way that was fruitful for human evolution.

We will now pass on to Sun evolution. After a period of rest Saturn changed into the form of Sun. Externally it is true to say that in the middle of the Sun period a condensation of its substance took place. Sun consisted not only of warmth, but also of gas and air (in the esoteric sense), and everything within Sun passed through its evolution under conditions only possible in warmth and air. To begin with, the following took place: when the human being consisted only of warmth he could not assume an etheric body; but now, on Sun, he became permeated by an etheric body, thus consisting of two principles: a physical body and an etheric body. The human physical body on Sun was, however, quite different to what it is now. Let us try to form an idea, if only a rough one, of the physical body upon Old Sun. Imagine that we have breathed in air and that the inhaled air has passed into us. This air is now permeated with a certain degree of warmth. Now think away everything but the inhaled air, which in effect forms an image of the whole human body; think away all the solid and the liquid parts, keeping only the air and the warmth in mind. You then have in imagination a form before you such as would appear if you considered merely the inhaled air and its activity. If you observed the form of this inhaled air and the warmth the human being contains you would have approximately the form the human being had at the middle of the Sun period.

If we have currents of warmth and, in addition to these, currents of gas which form the physical body, how does the clairvoyant see this gas in the Akashic Record? When the warmth condenses into air and no other conditions are present (as is the case now on earth, where the sun pours in from without), the moment this gas or air separates from the form of warmth it begins to shine. Hence upon Sun the physical body was a kind of germinal body of warmth, composed of gaseous or airy currents, which glittered in the most wonderful way and shone with varied colours. The entire Sun globe consisted of shining warmth bodies, which were the primary rudiments of our human physical bodies. On Sun the human being rose a stage higher, adding an etheric body to the physical body. It was the human being himself who, as part of the form of the Sun, radiated the illuminating power of light into space; his physical body, through taking the etheric body into itself, became luminous. The physical body was now at the second stage of its progress towards perfection, but the etheric body, which first became luminous on the Sun, was only at its first stage.

Following human evolution further, we find that Sun, after entering upon a period of rest, gradually passed over into the Moon incarnation. Materially, gaseous form condensed into the fluid element. The ancient Moon was in fact a fluid body, and within it you would again have found physical human bodies as plastic forms, consisting now of flowing sap, or watery constituents, in which currents of air coursed just as breath and warmth intermingle in our body today. The physical body now consisted of three aspects: water, gas or air, and warmth; and the etheric body which it had previously possessed now passed over with it into the Moon period. The human being was now in a position to assimilate an astral body, and from this time onwards he consisted of three principles: the physical body, the etheric body and the astral body.

During the Moon period it was not possible for all the beings connected with it to maintain the same rate of progress in their development. It was not only during the Earth stage of our evolution, but also earlier, during the Moon period, that the sun separated off from the common world-body; so that in the middle of the Moon period we have two spheres—the moon (earth plus moon) and the sun, which as you know had departed along with the most advanced of the spiritual beings. The withdrawal of the finer forces and higher beings left the grosser ones behind during Moon evolution; this planet therefore (earth plus moon) began to densify and harden. You must realize that even during Old Moon evolution the sun with its beings worked for a time from outside upon the less advanced body of the moon.

We now need to describe in more detail this body which had remained behind after the departure of the sun, for we underwent part of our evolution upon it. On Saturn there was only the physical human body, at the mineral stage. Upon Sun the human being raised himself to the vegetable stage, then possessing physical body and etheric body; but at this stage certain beings became retrograde, they did not rise as high as human-plant existence on Old Sun, but remained at the Saturn stage. These were the forerunners of certain animals of the present day. Our past reaches back to Old Saturn, whereas the forerunners of a certain portion of our present animal kingdom had their origin only on Sun as a second kingdom beside the human.

For the same reason, due to certain beings not advancing, when the human being had worked his way upward on Moon to a condition where he was the possessor of three principles, two other kingdoms surrounded him: one a kingdom which on Moon had remained behind at the stage of plants—the precursors of the animals of today—and one that was still at the stage of minerals, these last being the forerunners of our present plants. Our mineral kingdom did not as yet exist on Moon. It came into existence last, as a sort of deposit from the other kingdoms. Of course anyone who affirms such things knows very well that it seems nonsense in modern terms to say that plants could originate without the substrate of a mineral kingdom, but formerly conditions were entirely different. In fact, upon Old Moon human beings developed in a sense within the animal kingdom, animals within the vegetable kingdom, and plants within the mineral kingdom; and at the time when the moon body separated from the sun all the kingdoms shifted as follows:

1. The human kingdom (really animal kingdom, consisting of physical body, etheric, and astral bodies).
2. The animal kingdom (really vegetable kingdom, consisting of physical and etheric bodies).
3. The vegetable kingdom (really mineral kingdom, because it consisted only of a physical body).

In other words, our present mineral kingdom did not as yet exist. Now, when the moon and sun separated, the beings and forces of the sun were completely liberated from the gross material of the moon, so that they could act all the more strongly. The result was that all three kingdoms were raised a level higher. The human astral body was lifted out of its close connection with the lower principles, so that, compared with the human being with physical, etheric, and astral bodies at the beginning of the Moon period, one would later have perceived a change. Because the sun had departed and begun to shine from without, the astral and etheric bodies were partly liberated. The consequence was that something happened which we must try to picture in the following way. Imagine that the human being of today consisted only of physical body, etheric body and astral body, and that now an external force approached which drove out our etheric and astral bodies. To the clairvoyant these would now exist outside us, but through these two bodies being liberated from the weight of the physical body, the human being could be raised about half a level upward in evolution.

Something like this took place at the time of which I am speaking: the human being was lifted up to become a being midway between the present human being and present animal. In a spiritual sense he was, however, guided and directed by the exalted sun powers. In like manner the two other kingdoms were raised about half a level, so that around the middle of Moon evolution we do not find our present kingdoms, but intermediate ones: we have a human-animal kingdom, an animal-vegetable kingdom, and a vegetable-mineral kingdom.

Here on earth we walk upon a solid mineral ground; the beings of Old Moon walked on what was the lowest kingdom of that planet—the vegetable-mineral. This substrate of the Moon was not a mineral substance such as we have on the earth, but something that was half-alive. One has an approximate idea of what this basic substance of the Moon was if we think of something resembling a mossy bog or boiled spinach, a kind of mush, but living, bubbling. There were no rocks projecting out of this mass, but there was something like dense, woody, vegetable masses, horny structures; and these took the place of our present rocks. To clairvoyant vision it appears as if the human being moved upon a vegetable-mineral foundation which later underwent compression to become the rocks of today. Out of this substance grew the animal-plants. These were more or less firmly rooted; they were more mobile, it is true, than plants are now, but they grew out of this viscous element and had a certain degree of sensation when touched. The animal-human realm emerged from the finest substances, by no means reaching down into the grossest, but forming a physical body from the finest substances. This physical body, which was in a continual state of transformation, had a very strange appearance: the clairvoyant is unable to discern upon Old Moon a human head such as we possess today. Although the physical body was still soft and fluid, the clairvoyant perceives only animal-like heads, with etheric and astral bodies projecting beyond this animal head formation. To physical perception all these animal-people had various forms that recall our present animals, but they are only reminiscent of these; it is only when we rise from physical sight to astral vision that we perceive the higher nature of the animal-man of Moon evolution. Such were the denizens of Old Moon.

When we examine the course of human cultural development, in so far as it is of a spiritual nature, we find in many instances that the myths and legends that have been handed down to us are in many respects wiser than our modern science. When more is known about the spiritual foundations of the world people will recognize in many of the myths, legends, and fairy tales a truly deep wisdom, deeper than science, which is seemingly so advanced. Let us return for a moment to Old Moon, in whose substrate only those ancient animal-plants could flourish, and let us leave aside study of the further evolution of the Moon itself. We must clearly understand that all these Moon-beings were the forerunners of today's earth beings. Our present mineral kingdom has sprung from the vegetable-mineral of the Moon epoch, descending half a level lower; from the animal-plants have sprung our present plants; and most of our animals have originated from the animal-men who remained behind, who did not advance. Thus we see that our minerals, our plants, our animals and our human beings are really the descendants of the beings of Old Moon.

There is today a remarkable plant, mistletoe, which does not grow in a mineral soil. When observed clairvoyantly it is seen to be different from other plants, exhibiting rudiments of an astral body informing it in the same way as in animals. Although this plant has no sensation it has something resembling the outer form of animals. This is because it belongs to those backward plant-animals of the Moon period, which were unable to become plants, and on this account cannot thrive on a mineral soil, but require other plants on which to take root.

Mistletoe has preserved the condition of Old Moon. The ancestors of some of the European peoples knew this fact and embodied the knowledge in a wonderful legend.[11] The Germanic and Norse peoples recognized in Loki a power still belonging to those forces which passed from the field of activity on Old Moon to Earth. When the earth became Earth it fell under the influence of other forces, which these ancient peoples symbolized in the god Baldur. He represents all those forces which work upon mature earth beings; but those who had remained at the Moon stage felt an inner relationship to Loki, the Moon god. Hence arose the wonderful legend telling how once upon a time when the gods were playing, all creatures swore an oath that they would not injure Baldur; the mistletoe alone did not take this oath. Why? Because it is not related to the earth forces incarnated in Baldur, but is a retrograde Moon entity, and so has power to injure the earth forces fundamentally embodied in Baldur. Loki had to be served by a being belonging to himself. This legend has its origin deep in the hidden foundations of the world. And when we know that in many respects what is opposed to healthy development must be of service to unhealthy development, we understand the wise intuition of our forefathers which led them to look to the mistletoe for special curative forces and juices. They knew that of which we have just spoken, hence the role they gave to the mistletoe. From this example we can see that profound wisdom regarding the evolution of the world is frequently hidden in myth and legend.

Through the withdrawal of a part of the etheric and astral body of the animal-man upon Old Moon the necessity arose, even at that time, for a change of consciousness. But we must first speak of another development which ran parallel with this. Each of the planetary stages of development—on Saturn, Sun, Moon, and Earth—was at the same time a stage in the development of consciousness. Upon Saturn, at the first level, consciousness was dim. Such consciousness as we have in dreamless sleep—the consciousness possessed by eternally sleeping plants—is clearer than what human beings possessed upon Saturn, which may be compared to the consciousness of minerals. Only on Sun did human beings rise to a consciousness like that possessed by plants. Then on Moon, through the astral body they received, their consciousness rose one degree higher, to what we can call picture-consciousness. This may be compared in a certain sense with our present dream-consciousness, although our dreams have deeper meaning only in exceptional cases. Upon Moon this was different: the pictures which rose and disappeared signified something. When another being approached, the human being was unable to perceive its outer form and colour, but instead perceived something which rose within himself (much as is now the case in dreams); a picture rose within him of the inner nature of the approaching being, and in accordance with the colour and character of this picture he knew whether this being was friendly towards him or the reverse—whether he should remain or flee.

As stated, a change of consciousness took place upon Moon after the sun had departed from it: there were periods of alternating consciousness, times when consciousness was more vivid, and times when it was dimmer. Today we have interchanging periods of day and night. In the morning we draw into our physical body and etheric body, and the external world with its beings and objects rises before us. Everything around us becomes light and clear because we make use of our senses, but at night when our I and astral body emerge, we have no instrument to perceive with and everything is dark around us. Dreamless sleep consciousness, which the human being first acquired on Sun, now alternates with waking, earth consciousness. These conditions were already prepared on Old Moon. At that time the etheric and astral bodies were not continuously outside us; there were periods when they sank into our physical body, for the planetary body of Old Moon already rotated around the sun, and this brought about conditions in which the sun shone upon us at certain times, and not at others. This led to the etheric and astral bodies entering and departing from the physical body. The change was certainly not as strongly contrasted as at present.

During the periods of the withdrawal of these bodies on Moon, when solar forces shone upon the human being, he was in a clear, spiritual consciousness, clearly perceiving what was spiritual. When his etheric and astral bodies sank back into the physical body his consciousness became darkened. You see, it was the reverse of present conditions.

For long, long periods of time, alternating states of clear and dim consciousness occurred upon Moon, and it was in the dim state of consciousness that, without the human being's awareness, what we call fertilization took place. For powers of reproduction to be developed, so that the human being might bring forth his kind, his higher being had to sink down into the physical body, and once this had been accomplished it rose again into the higher world. At that time preparation was gradually made for what has since been fully developed upon earth. Through the separation of the sun, because of it having empowered and invigorated its creatures, the human being along with all the other creatures and entities was able to evolve to a higher degree. If solar forces had been inhibited for a longer period by Old Moon, they could not have acted so powerfully; but once they were released from the hindrance of Moon-substances, Moon and all its denizens advanced rapidly. After a time Moon had attained such maturity that it could again be absorbed by the sun. This was followed by a condition when all the planets which had been separated could also be again absorbed, when they all re-entered the spiritual state of rest which we call pralaya. After this pause there came forth once more what we may call the first etheric germs of the Earth body, out of which at a later period everything was again differentiated. But let us ask this: Where does each body come from, the physical body on Saturn, the etheric body on Sun, and the astral body on Moon?

Pupils of spiritual science do not pursue questions of origin into a more and more abstract realm in a philosophically inept way.

This is only done as long as the inquirer has not risen to a spiritual observation of the world. Reasonably, one must come at last to a point where the significance of questions ceases. One might ask: Whence come these furrows on the road? The answer is: A cart passed this way. Then comes the further question: Whence came the cart? And one might answer: A person on certain business was using it. They then ask: What kind of business? At length the questions become meaningless or arrive in quite different realms. If the purpose of the enquiry starts with an idea, one only arrives at endless further abstract questions. But in tangible observations one arrives at last at spiritual beings, and then one no longer asks, *Why* are they doing this? But instead: *What* are they doing? It is important to school oneself to recognize the limitations of questions.

Esoteric observation reveals that in the beginning, when Old Saturn began to be formed, certain spiritual beings poured forth the fundamental substance of Saturn—warmth—from their own substance as a sacrifice. They had matured so far that they did not need to absorb anything as nourishment; they were even in a position to sacrifice themselves to pour out their own substance. These beings are the thrones. It is they who through their sacrifice formed the foundations of the human physical body. Someone who can esoterically observe the physical body on Saturn can say that it streamed forth from the substance of the thrones. The physical body changes from stage to stage, it develops ever higher, but what we bear within us is always the transformed substance of the thrones.

Then we pass on to Old Sun. Here the etheric body was added to the physical body. Here again are spiritual beings, at a lower level than the thrones, whom we call spirits of wisdom, kyriotetes. They did not develop far enough on Saturn to be able to pour out their own being, but on Sun they had progressed far enough, and there now streamed from them the substance of the etheric body. Since the Sun period our etheric bodies bear within them the substance of the spirits of wisdom.

On the Moon the astral body was added to us. Here again there were spiritual beings who sacrificed their substance. These were the spirits of motion, dynamis. Lastly we pass from the Moon to the

Earth stage. Here other beings pour their force into us—we receive the I. To the three members we already possess the I is now added. This is bestowed on us by the spirits of form or exusiai: these are the Elohim, who give to us their sunlight, also Jehovah, who, from the moon, gives form to the human spirit. Herein we see the cooperation of the two categories of the spirits of form who, from without, endow us with the rudiments of our I.

Thus we find that from stage to stage spiritual beings incorporate themselves into human evolution: on Saturn the thrones; on Sun the kyriotetes; on Moon the dynamis; and on Earth the exusiai—Jehovah and the Elohim. From all these beings we human beings have received our present shape and form: they have allowed their own being to pour into us. In the Bible we are clearly shown how the being of one of the spirits of form streamed into the human being. Profound secrets lie behind what is found in the Torah.[12] Consider that one of the spirits of form united with the moon as Jehovah, that from there he worked as a spirit of form upon the human being, and, bestowing on him what gave to him his divine form, 'God made the human being in his own likeness.' He gave to him the form of the gods. The spirits of form endowed us with the human form, that is, the divine form. The Elohim poured sun powers as light upon the earth. The god Jehovah renounced the outer form, the outer garment of light; he streamed to earth as a dark god, limiting himself to the period between birth and death. Through the air, which the light permeates, the spirits of air made themselves his companions. If we wish to form a picture of what streams physically and spiritually from the sun to the earth we have to see the sun's rays absorbed by the earth and borne toward the human being, bringing with them also what streams to us from the Jehovah spirit, as well as what lives spiritually in the air.

The moment when Jehovah poured forth a part of his powerful being is indicated in the Bible in the words: 'God breathed the breath of life into man, and he became a living soul.'[13] Such a statement ought to be taken quite literally, and we must try to understand what it really contains. A thrill of awe pervades us when we begin to understand such a statement, and when we learn its meaning; telling as it does that after the thrones, the spirits of will, on Saturn, the spirits of wisdom on Sun, the spirits of motion on the Moon, had poured their principles into the human being, then—on Earth—the spirits of form imbued him. It is this mighty moment that is referred to in words of the Bible quoted above.

In the next lecture we shall learn further of the Elohim and Jehovah, and how they cooperated with luciferic beings throughout the Atlantean epoch and on into our own.

Lecture 6

STUTTGART, 10 AUGUST 1908

The Spirits of Form as Regents of Earthly Existence

It belongs to the very nature of our theme that these lectures should proceed in a particular way, that we should approach our goal, as it were, in circles; that starting from the broader circumference we should describe ever smaller circles to reach what we seek. Hence it may seem in the beginning as if there were no system in our observations, but by gradually approaching the inner from without we shall arrive at a right understanding of the whole.

In our last lecture we reached a point where we found that the spirits of form, or exusiai as they are called in Christian esotericism, are the specific regents of human earth existence. The heart of the matter is contained in the fact that these spirits of form worked in the course of earthly evolution both into the substance and into the soul nature of the human being. At a certain point of time they reached such a high stage of development that they could no longer make use of the earth as a field of action but, drawing with them the finer forces and substances, they left the earth and formed a new field for their activities on our sun.

What do we mean when we say that the spirits of form are the specific regents of earthly existence? Were these spirits not already active in the earlier planetary stages of evolution, during Saturn, Sun, and Moon epochs? Yes, they certainly were, but they had then a different field of activity to what they have on the earth. This can be understood when we consider the facts already presented. Upon Saturn the rudiments of the physical body alone existed; neither the etheric nor the astral body had as yet poured into it. Of course the spirits of form, of whom Jehovah is one, were active even at that time; but, to use a mundane expression, they did not yet have such a well-prepared foundation on which to work. Only through the spirits of wisdom giving the human being an etheric body on Sun, and the spirits of motion giving him an astral body on Moon, did the spirits of form find a sufficiently prepared human being on which they could work on Earth. For only when the human being possessed a physical, etheric and astral body could the spirits of form give him what we now know as the human form. The form you are able to observe in yourselves today existed at no earlier stage of evolution. The conditions that were present on Moon, Sun and Saturn were preparatory stages; everything had first to undergo a certain development before the human being could rise to his present noble form. If asked why the spirits of form could not set to work on Saturn we must reply: because the germinal rudiments of the physical body were then too immature; a certain state of maturity had first to come about. This maturity was only reached at the time when our earth, together with the sun, formed one planet of a very fine substance. The spirits of form were active even then, working slowly and gradually upon the human body. We can point to the period when this fashioning of the human being came to a certain conclusion, when the human form was, in a way, finished. This was not the case in the first part of the Atlantean epoch.

If you go back to a time long before the great catastrophe swept Atlantis away we find our ancestors in a condition very different from our own. It was only about the middle of the Atlantean epoch that the human being received a form essentially the same as we possess today. Before then his material parts were softer. We find the human being consisting of a soft substance having no trace of our present hard bones, nothing even so solid as cartilage. He swam in the air, which was still permeated by dense fluid; he was a kind of water being, such as certain medusae are today that can hardly be distinguished from the surrounding water. At that time the forces of human bone structure were organized, but the bones themselves had not hardened, and the connection between the higher and the lower principles of the human being was very different to what it is now.

We know that when we are asleep today our physical and etheric body lie on the bed, while our astral body and I are outside it. As the etheric body is nowadays approximately the same in size and form as the physical body, we are also quickly free from it when we withdraw with our astral body from the physical body. This was not so in the first part of the Atlantean epoch; the etheric body then projected on all sides beyond the physical body, especially the head. The consequence of this was that when the astral body withdrew it always remained connected with the etheric body. In human beings today, the moment the astral body leaves the physical body it has also left the etheric body. The consequence of the former connection between the astral body and the etheric body was that, when the physical vehicle had been left behind, the human being at night was not surrounded and pervaded by such darkness and lack of consciousness as is the case today. Back then, when outside his physical body, he could perceive soul-spiritual beings with his dim clairvoyance. It is as if when your astral body withdrew on going to sleep, and your vision was turned away from the physical world, a world appeared in its place that was peopled with soul-spiritual beings.

The early Atlanteans had no use for a solid skeleton, and as the physical body was soft it was also pliable. This is something which clairvoyant consciousness can see as having actually existed, outrageous as it may seem to modern materialistic consciousness. During the Atlantean period, the human being had great power over the shape of his body. If he wished a part of his body, say that which later became a hand, to assume a different form, to be elastically lengthened, for example, he could do this; he had power not only to move his limbs, but to lengthen them; he could, as it were, inflate himself. This was actually possible at the time we are speaking of: he could extend and lengthen his fingers. We find this more particularly the case when we go back to the Lemurian epoch. I will ask you now to note a connection between two things. When did the human being lose the power to lengthen and contract his limbs? At the time the spirits of form completed the elaboration of his form. As long as the human being's physical form—the form he was to retain—had not been perfected, other spirits could govern him, and he could change his shape. So that if we go back to the period preceding the Atlantean epoch we find that the human being had no definite form, but a continually changing one. We have to realize that there came a point of time when the spirits of form had finished all they had to do in order to make the human form resemble their own, for it was their own shape they gave to the human being.

Let us now suppose that certain human beings had not been able to wait until the point of time referred to when the spirits of form had finished their work. Such beings would have hardened at some earlier stage of development, their form would, to a certain extent, have ossified, thus preserving some earlier form. It was, however, necessary that the being who was to become human should keep his shape pliable, supple until the right moment came for it to assume a fixed form.

Let us briefly consider a period lying very far back, for here we are dealing with vast periods of time when our external being was of such a nature that it had constant need of the forces that worked upon it to remodel and ennoble it. Suppose that, through events which we will consider later, certain human beings had partly freed themselves from the ever-active forces of form, that they were no longer so entirely pervaded by these forces as they had been. Such human beings would in this case have remained at some previous stage. This did indeed happen: the beings which freed themselves too early and did not allow the spirits of form to complete their work are those that most closely resemble us—the apes. They could not wait; they did not remain long enough in the bosom of those divine beings whom we call the spirits of form. What occurred in the case of the apes was continually happening with other creatures; again and again some beings remained behind and became hardened in form.

It was thus that the whole range of today's animal kingdom arose.

But if you ask if human beings originated from such animal forms, the answer is no. The human being remained above the surface of the earth in purer elements, and only solidified when the time was ripe for him to do so. This point of time when the human being descended to earth from spiritual heights, is beautifully portrayed in the Bible in the legend of Paradise. In spite of all investigations, the place of Paradise is not to be found upon earth, but above it. The human being only descended from Paradise to earth after receiving his final, definite form.

What ought to have happened in the middle of the Atlantean epoch when the spirits of form had finished their fashioning of the physical body? The human being should have been able to perceive his environment with his senses, which would then have been perfected; he should have lived for the first time with his external physical environment. Up to that time everything about him had indefinite outlines; only then could he enter into relationship with the external world in what we may call the normal way. Only then could he have learned to distinguish himself from other objects; for he only then had a physical body which could be considered a suitable vehicle for his I. We have already said that certain beings had remained behind at every stage of evolution. Not all of them had reached the stage they might have reached, not even all the beings whom we have called the spirits of form; and it is these backward beings who enter most essentially into all considerations about the evolution of the human being on earth.

We have already said that besides the exalted beings working from the sun and moon there are others, dwelling on Mercury and Venus, the celestial bodies lying between the sun and earth, who are at an intermediate stage between the human being and the lofty sun and moon spirits. The sun spirits had achieved their rightful development, and at precisely the point of time were able to work in the right way. But there were other beings, situated between the earth and the sun spirits, who did not find this point of time, and because they were outside the course of normal development they were active at other times. What was the result of this? Think once more of the course of human evolution. Let us recall yet again that the human being consists of physical body, etheric body, astral body and I. We know that the task of the I is to transform our other principles, starting by gradually bringing the astral body under control; this means that human beings must learn to control their passions and impulses. The time had come when the I should appear in the human being and proceed to work upon the astral body, when the astral body was to be gradually transformed and the spirit-self developed. The first possibility of this work of transformation was when the spirits of form became active in the middle of the Atlantean epoch.

But we must now try to understand the remarkable role at that time of the retrograde beings. They had not progressed far enough to assist the human being in the development of the spirit-self, consequently they worked upon his astral body, which had not yet progressed far enough to receive the I. Thus, there was a time in the evolution of earthly humanity when the undeveloped astral body was exposed to the influence of these backward spiritual beings. You will understand this better if you remember that on Old Moon the human being had only a physical, etheric and astral body, and at that time the spirits of form worked in the normal course of things upon his astral body. These beings, who meanwhile had evolved further, now worked normally upon the I, while the retrograde ones continued to work upon the astral body as they had done during Moon evolution. Thus before the human I arose, these retrograde but still lofty beings worked upon the human astral body. We call these beings after their leader—luciferic beings. Two kinds of beings, therefore, worked upon us: the normally working spirits of form, of whom we have spoken, and these luciferic beings who had not advanced sufficiently to be able to work upon the I, and who had already been working on the astral body. These latter beings, therefore, retarded human development: if they had not worked upon us at the time we would have been sufficiently advanced by the middle of the Atlantean epoch for the spirits of form to work upon our I.

Can what the retrograde spirits did to the human being—as compared with what the exalted, rightfully active spirits did—be termed 'bad' in a trivial sense? No, certainly not. If we consider the facts which clairvoyant vision is able to study, we find that in reality these retrograde spirits accelerated human evolution. The human being would have had to wait until the very last eras for the development of certain capacities, whereas through the action of these beings he gained them earlier. Through the action of the luciferic beings, therefore, the human being received certain qualities of mind and spirit before the destined time, thus rising to a certain higher stage of mental and spiritual development. This was not wrong, but, curious as it may seem, something which even in a higher sense indicates infinitely wise guidance in the progressive evolution of humanity. Through attaining at a lower stage certain capacities which were otherwise only destined for human beings in the middle of the Atlantean epoch, they came to them in an entirely different, self-aware and free manner. The human being would have been tied by spiritual apron strings up to the middle of the Atlantean epoch if these retrograde beings had not intervened. How, then, must we regard their backward state? Looked at superficially, one might easily think of them as one thinks of pupils who have to repeat a year at school. These spirits are not, however, backward due to laziness, but they remained behind because they were willing to sacrifice themselves. They sacrificed themselves so as to give the human being the possibility of receiving the gifts of the spirits of form in a higher way—in a free way.

There was a long period in human evolution when, through these luciferic beings, humanity received the first beginnings of speech and of thought, especially of thinking memory, received the rudimentary germ of art and of science. Human beings could not have attained this previously, for they would then have acquired it merely as an instinctive activity. Through this something else came within their domain, something which, under the guidance of the spirits of form, would have passed them by; they were exposed to the possibility of straying from the right path—exposed to good and evil. Without the intervention of the luciferic beings the human being would never have been exposed to this; but this also happened for the sake of freedom. Because the luciferic beings accelerated a part of our evolution they brought freedom to us at an earlier age. We all bear within us the seeds of the work of the luciferic spirits.

By the middle of the Atlantean epoch the spirits of form had perfected their development to a degree that enabled them to endow the human being with what they themselves possessed. The human being would have received the complete, germinal I at this time if these spirits alone had worked on him, but luciferic beings had been active from an earlier period, and had accelerated evolution considerably: upward on the one hand, and downward on the other. Through this something else of great importance came about.

If evolution had proceeded without the luciferic beings, the human being would have attained a certain maturity by the middle of the Atlantean epoch but without the possibility of freedom. Through no merit of his own, the human being would have become mature enough to receive the gift of the spirits of form. Now that luciferic beings had endowed him with an earlier maturity, this also brought with it a certain deterioration, and on this account not all the higher sun powers nor all the forces of the spirits of form were able to work upon him at this period. This leads to something important. If human beings had reached the middle of the Atlantean epoch merely with a higher spiritual instinct, without freedom, and, therefore, without any merit of their own, they would already have been sufficiently mature for the descent to earth of that principle which we call the Christ principle; the Christ would already have appeared then. Freedom had, however, been given to humankind, which had thereby been pushed down below the stage of normal, instinctual development. Human beings therefore now had to become mature by their own powers, so that they might later be able to receive the Christ principle. We must clearly understand that the descent of Christ and his work was retarded by the intervention of the luciferic beings, but through this intervention mankind had a mature form when the Christ ultimately did descend.

From this we see that it was luciferic beings who made human beings what they are today, and who prepared them for the great event of the descent of the Christ principle. It is as if the luciferic beings said this: If we leave the human being in such a condition that he progresses into the Atlantean epoch in an instinctive way only, he will receive the Christ principle also instinctively. He will not be free, not mature in freedom. We will therefore sacrifice ourselves; we will develop in human beings certain capacities and qualities, thus delaying the moment when they can see the Christ. Luciferic beings began their work as long before the middle of the Atlantean epoch as Christ appeared after it.

If we now ask what these luciferic powers gave human beings, and what they were therefore able to receive already in the middle of the Atlantean epoch, we find that they received something which could come to them only from without, which they could not yet attain through their own soul. On this account everything which came to them from the spirits of form, who had worked on them previously, was such that it did not flow from their own innermost being; human beings followed an outer impulse, rather: they obeyed laws.

Just as the animal has to follow instinctively the laws implanted in it, so Jehovah gave laws to man. He gave the 'law' which was then realized outwardly by Moses and the prophets. Meanwhile human beings matured toward receiving within themselves the motives and impulses for their actions. And so we see that, without the human being's participation, powers prepare the nature of their life on earth. Where, then, do these powers work? They work principally where, as we can say, the blood comes into its own: in reproduction, and in all that is connected with it. In ancient times we find gods and folk spirits, or group spirits, working within tribes and communities through ordering laws. There we find that what is related by blood loves its own; it loves because love is implanted by the laws of nature; and the further back we go the more we find that all those related by blood consider themselves as belonging to one another. Everything loves those attributes that love has implanted in it through natural laws and outer formative forces. Jehovah worked in the forces of blood relationship; hence the feeling of belonging one to another. Jehovah produced order and harmony through the relationship that is connected with the blood, and those who opposed him were the luciferic beings, who directed their strongest attacks against the principle of blood relationship. Up to the time of the coming of Christ, they continually sought to centre the human being within his own personality and sunder him from blood relationship. Then the Christ appears and, endowing human beings with his inward power, centres them entirely within their own personality making wisdom and grace the inmost impulses of their being.

The luciferic beings had prepared the human being for this through very long periods of time. Only at the time of Christ's coming were human beings ready for what these luciferic beings desired. Those who uttered the words *Christus versus Luciferus*,[14] Christ the true Lucifer, knew well what they were saying. This is an esoteric statement.

We have seen that two principles were in fact continually at work in those olden times we call pre-Christian; there was a binding principle which worked through blood relationship, and a sundering principle which sought to centre human beings in their own personality. We can see how the whole of humanity was fashioned under the influence of these two principles.

Let us picture a certain stage of human evolution in the Atlantean epoch when humankind was approaching the time of its subsequent hardening into the skeleton's bony form. The spirits guiding the human being had now to ensure that the bones should not harden too quickly. For a considerable length of time in Atlantean evolution the human skeleton needed to remain soft enough for it to be transformed. As we know, however, beings remained behind at every stage, and certain groups of human beings remained behind at an early period because the bony system grew too hard prematurely. The principle of form prevailed here, holding a group of human beings in the form they had then attained. What was the consequence? Forms may be hardened and held back, but evolution as a whole goes forward, so that forms which have thus been held back artificially arrive later in a time to which they are no longer suited. A time came when there was less moisture in the air, when climatic conditions changed and were no longer suitable for those who had remained behind.

Groups of human beings in whom the bones had, as it were, become too pronounced, were now left behind. They could not adapt to post-Atlantean conditions. Such peoples had degenerated. There were other backward groups in whom not only the skeletal system but also the system that sustains nutrition hardened too early—the system governed by the forces of the etheric body whereas the skeletal system is governed by forces of the physical body. Then there are those who degenerated because the nervous system became hardened, not remaining soft long enough for it to become available as an instrument of higher thought, hence certain drives and instincts, certain tendencies to sensual instincts resulted. Lastly, we have those in whom at a certain stage the I hardened within itself; it hardened in the blood which is the outward expression of the I. But those who kept the above elements supple, so that they did not remain fixed or hardened, but were always able to develop further and even overcome the enclosing of the I, formed that human group which journeyed from the regions now covered by the Atlantic Ocean into the Europe and Asia of today.

Connected with this we find the following remarkable fact: from the Atlantean continent departed several migratory streams of human beings who, having hardened in various ways, went in different directions; those in whom the bones had hardened journeyed westward, and their last descendants were found when America was discovered. Those whose nutritional system had hardened went principally to Africa; others (the Malays) went towards Asia. Then there are those who formed the ancestors of the Mongolian race. The last to migrate were those who dwelt in the neighbourhood of the Ireland of today; those who had kept themselves pliant and unformed the longest. These wandered from the West towards the East, and left behind them certain communities of people all over the Continent of Europe. The most advanced journeyed towards Asia, and there mingled in various ways with others who had come by different routes.

Let us now think of a period that is not as ancient, an age when people still possessed dim clairvoyance, and when initiates still possessed great influence; an age when consciousness still existed of the facts which have just been mentioned. How did this consciousness find expression? In Ancient Greece, those who possessed this awareness found a people who had hardened sooner than themselves: and to their South they found a race which had originated through mixing with others, that had hardened in a still earlier condition. This lived in the awareness of the Greeks. When the Greeks looked backwards over the course of their past evolution, they said this: I look towards Africa, and there I find in the Egyptian age advanced human beings who had been influenced by previous ages of civilization (the Babylonian-Chaldean); still earlier there was a people in this region among whom existed a strong tendency towards hardening relative to those qualities which reached down into the lower nature of the nutritional principle. Another stage developed later when this people had come into contact with those migrating from Asia. Besides these were others who had kept themselves supple the longest.

In the sculptured forms of their gods, the Greeks idealized their knowledge of human evolution, which they saw to be the outcome of active, divine forces. They knew that at a very early stage certain human beings had hardened, and that others had preserved their suppleness and pliability. Then they considered themselves, seeing that in certain ways they were indeed backward, but they belonged to those who had kept supple and plastic the longest. All this is wonderfully portrayed in Greek sculpture. If we examine it carefully we find three types of gods:

1. The Zeus type, to which belong the whole circle of gods around Zeus.
2. The Hermes or Mercury type. This was added later to the Zeus type, and was portrayed by the Greeks as an entirely distinct form. If you observe the type of hair of Zeus and his kind, and, on the other hand the curly hair of Hermes, also the form of the eyes and the position of the ears, you will see that the Greeks wished to express something different by this.
3. The Satyr type, belonging to a still older humanity, in turn clearly distinguished from the Mercury type.

We here have something which the Greeks wished to express in their particular fashion. What lay to their South they expressed in the Satyr type. What lay to their East they associated with the Hermes type; and what might be called their own kind, they expressed in the sublime, noble Zeus type. Anyone who wishes can see in all these forms how beautifully the Greek adapted what lives in external form to the inward formative forces. I will point to one more detail which shows how refined the Greek artists were in their efforts to give expression, in artistic forms, to great world conceptions. Observe for a moment the Asiatic type embodied in the form of Hermes. Because it had remained at the stage of lower human forces, the prominent forces active in this type, giving form to the face, were those that hold sway in the lower part of the human being. On the other hand, the forces belonging to the type of the Greeks themselves worked in higher aspects. This can be seen most characteristically in Zeus, in the noble shape of the forehead.

The distinctive consciousness of the Greeks worked into the plastic forms of their art, and we can only understand what has arisen in the course of evolution when we observe these active forces and see how the artists formed such details as the eyes, for example. Besides our appreciation of the subtle observation of the Greek artists, we discover in the distinctive forms of what they produced artistically their recognition of how inner formative forces had shaped external form. We recognize how racial attributes were embodied in the figures of Greek mythology, and we see how the diverse forms of Greek art uniquely embody those active spiritual forces, right down to such details as the shape of an eye.

Lecture 7

STUTTGART, 11 AUGUST 1908

Animal Forms as the Physiognomy of Human Passions

In the last lecture we saw how a differentiation had arisen in evolution generally, and particularly in human evolution, because human beings, and other beings also, could not await the right point in their evolution; they therefore fell behind and became hardened to a certain degree, while others retained the necessary softness and pliability until the right moment, and were thus able to initiate the necessary transformations. We also saw that it was only in the middle of the Atlantean epoch that the true human form appeared. In the previous epoch, and indeed at a very early period, the external form of the human being was very mobile; not only could we move our limbs as at present, but through inner powers we could enlarge or extend them, etc. To the ordinary consciousness of today it seems a kind of outrage to say such things about past conditions of the earth and human being. Even here among anthroposophists you may have observed that we endeavour to develop certain truths by small stages; we present them gradually, in small doses—they are then more easily assimilated.

Let us turn our attention once more to these early evolutionary developments. The Atlantean epoch also had a beginning, and it came to an end through mighty water catastrophes of a very complicated kind. The Atlantean epoch lasted for a long, a very long, time. When we go back still further we come to other catastrophes in the course of evolution, which may be called volcanic in nature, when large tracts of land lying south of Asia, east of Africa, and north of Australia went under. On these tracts of land humanity had dwelt, and, to borrow a term from natural science, the land was called the Lemurian continent. At that time human beings had a body much softer and more plastic than it is now. This was a period when the human being could assume many different shapes, which, if we were to describe them, would seem very grotesque to modern minds. We arrive here at a point of time before which human beings had as yet no kind of feeling of personality, no feeling of selfhood. They possessed no self-awareness, and, since their shape was still very mobile and unfinished, this outward form altered according to their emotions, being one thing at one time and something quite different at another: in this way it betrayed and expressed their inner being. Depending on whether their thoughts and passions were good or bad, their external shape assumed a different form. It was impossible at that time to entertain an evil thought and keep it hidden, for the external bodily form immediately expressed it. The human being therefore appeared in all kinds of shapes. There were at this time very few of the higher kinds of animals; the earth was peopled by the lower animals and the human being. And if one were companionable—and such indeed we all were fundamentally—one could find one's fellow human being through the expression they gave to this or that thought, or to this or that passion. What really are all such expressions? What are the physiognomic expressions of passions and thoughts? They are the shapes or forms of animals. When we observe the form of animals we see in the higher orders of the animal kingdom nothing but thoughts and passions of all sorts worked into a great tapestry. Everything that moves within the human astral body today, and remains hidden, was such a strong force at that time that it imparted at once to the soft body, which really consisted only of fire-mist, the shape which expressed that passion. A large number of our higher animals of today are in fact human beings who became so entangled in their passions that they grew hardened in these forms and fell behind in evolution. Anyone who observes their environment with true esoteric perception can express this feeling approximately as follows: In the course of becoming an ego or I, I have passed through what I now see in lions and snakes; I lived in all these forms, for in my inner being I experienced the qualities which are expressed in these animal shapes.

Those human beings capable of an ascending evolution, who maintained their inner core, found a certain balance, so that they possess the *capacity* for these passions, which are, however, of a soul nature only, and do not assume or acquire external form. This is what our higher development means. In animals we see our own past, although these have not the same form as that in which they appeared in past ages, for millions of years have passed since then. Let us assume that passions such as are now found in lions were manifest at that time in the outward form of a human being, giving him the semblance of a lion, that this form then hardened, and the genus lion originated. Since that time, however, the genus lion has also passed through further development, and because of this the present lion no longer has the same form as it did then. The present lion is the descendant of a genus that branched off from the human long ages ago. In the various animals we have, in a certain sense, to see our degenerate descendants; and this should help us to look with understanding upon the world around us.

We must not, however, imagine that all the animal forms we see around us, which represent certain conditions of hardening, are the result of evil human passions. Passions were necessary; the human being had to experience them in order that he might absorb from them into his own nature all that was useful. And so, when we look back into such periods of the earth's evolution we find in our environment animal shapes that are in a state of material metamorphosis. These are the expressions of passions, and working into such creatures we find those spiritual beings with whom we have become acquainted in previous lectures. We have to think of the earth as being still of a soft substance, and spiritual beings working upon this substance, and forming the various animal-like shapes.

Let us now recall that the Egyptian religion repeated the realities of the third epoch of the earth, preserving the results of it as religious knowledge. The Egyptian form of religion contained as knowledge what had taken place at one time on earth. You will now wonder no longer that so many animal and animal-headed shapes appeared in Egyptian art. This was a spiritual repetition of what had actually existed on the earth at one time, and was more than a mere allegory.

In a certain sense it is literally true when we say that the souls who principally incarnated in Egyptian bodies remembered the Lemurian epoch, and that their religion was spiritually a reborn memory of it.

Thus epoch after epoch of the earth is born again within human souls in the various religious conceptions through which the world passes. Even at a period later than this, the environment of the human being was absolutely different from what it is now, and, of course, the conditions of consciousness were essentially different. We must clearly understand that from the Lemurian epoch to the middle of the Atlantean epoch the present human form was only gradually fashioned. By the middle of the Atlantean epoch, in the normal course of its evolution, it had reached a certain degree of perfection through Jehovah and the spirits of form. Throughout this period—from the Lemurian epoch to the Atlantean epoch—was first formed the entirety of what we find in the human being today. The human being of Lemuria, had we been able to see him clairvoyantly, would have presented an enigma of a different order, for functions which today are separate were still united in him in a certain way. For example, when the Lemurian evolution was in its prime neither a breathing system nor a digestive and nutritional system existed as we now possess these. Substances were quite different; respiration and nutrition were in a certain sense connected, and performed one common function which was only later separated. The human being absorbed a kind of watery, milky substance, and this supplied him simultaneously with what he now acquires separately in the processes of respiration and nutrition.

Another thing was also not yet separated. We know that in the course of the period with which we are dealing the senses first opened to the outer world. Our senses did not yet perceive external objects at that time. The human being was limited to a picture-consciousness: vivid dream pictures rose within him, but there was no external consciousness of objects. On the other hand, as the first heralding of outer life—the first inkling of outer sense perception—human beings acquired the capacity to distinguish heat and cold in their environment. This was the very first beginning of sense perception on the earth, for human beings of that time still moved within the fluid element, but they now knew whether they were approaching a warm place or a cold one. This was made possible by an organ which they possessed at that time and which has since atrophied.

You will have heard that within the human brain there is an organ called the pineal gland; today it is atrophied, but formerly it opened outward. It was an energy-emitting organ from which rays issued. The human being moved about in the watery element with a kind of lantern which developed a certain light. This lantern, when the pineal gland was developed, projected from the head, enabling the human being to distinguish different degrees of warmth. It was the first generalized sense organ. Natural science describes it as an atrophied eye. This it never was; it was an organ of warmth, and could in fact perceive not only in its immediate environment, but also at a distance. Besides this it also had another task.

This organ, which closed when the other senses opened, was in certain ancient periods an organ of fertilization, so that sense-perception and fertilization were associated at one time. Through this organ the human being absorbed into himself from his environment the forces which made him capable of bringing forth his kind. At one particular period, when the moon was still one with the earth, the atmosphere of the earth was able, when the sun was in a certain position, to furnish the substance which caused this organ to shine with special luminosity. There actually were periods (and certain fishes which at times develop a light remind us of them) when general human fertilization occurred; times when, due to a particular position of the sun, the as yet entirely ungendered human being could produce his kind. Sense-perception and fertilization, nutrition and breathing, were intimately connected in the primeval past. The various organs were differentiated gradually, and very gradually the human being acquired the form we now possess. Through this the human being became ever more able to develop self-mastery, and what we call ego-consciousness. But all through the period when he moved through the earth's atmosphere guided by his perception of warmth he was under the influence of higher beings. It was principally the forces of the sun (which had already left the earth) working upon the earth's atmosphere that stimulated the organ of self-awareness. On the other hand, there was another organ which was specially stimulated through the moon-forces (both before and after it withdrew from the earth). This is situated in another part of the brain, and is usually called the mucous gland. Today this organ has no particular duty, formerly it regulated the lower functions, those of nutrition and respiration, which originally were one. With this mucous gland were connected all the inner forces by which the human being could enlarge or inflate himself and assume various shapes—everything by which he could voluntarily alter his form. Those alterations which were less voluntary depended on the other organ, the pineal gland.

From this we see how the human being has changed, and how, by obtaining a solid, definite form, he has separated himself from the beings acting on and influencing him from without to render him an instinctive being. All this gives us a clearer idea of the processes in human evolution which led at length to that condition when, in the middle of the Atlantean epoch, humankind had sufficiently matured for the outer world to act and impinge upon the sense organs, so that human beings could form judgements about the outer world. Until that time judgement had flowed into us from without. What we might call a kind of thinking flowed into us, somewhat as is the case with animals today. We have to bear in mind that humanity progressed irregularly, one portion entered into a condition of hardening earlier, another later, and we have already seen the various kinds of human forms that developed. We saw how certain human beings became stunted in their development by allowing this hardening process to take place too soon, by assuming some particular shape too soon, and how through this the different races developed. Only those people who migrated from their origins in the neighbourhood of Ireland were really mature enough to be receptive to what the earth had to offer to their outward sight; and as they travelled from the West to the East they populated the various countries they passed through in which remnants of those people were found who had taken other routes. With these they mingled, and from this union the various civilizations originated, while from those who migrated least far have sprung the European civilizations.

In order to complete our preliminary studies we must first turn to the greater cosmos and then again to the earth itself. We have explained human evolution in connection with the animals, and shown how humankind thrust them away and left them behind at an earlier stage of evolution. There is, of course, a great difference in animals—a certain important evolutionary boundary between the higher and the lower forms. Remember that as the human being evolved he gradually thrust aside the animal forms, and that he had only a very fine etheric form at the time when earth and sun were still united. When these separated he thrust from him certain animal forms, and these have remained behind at the stage in evolution which corresponds to the time when the sun was still within the earth. From these, entirely different forms have naturally arisen in the course of time, for we are here concerned with a very long subsequent evolutionary period. Were we to select a characteristic form which is still to be found today, and which may in some way be compared with those which remained behind when the earth was thrust away by the sun, we must come upon the form of the fish. This is the form which remained over when the earth was thrown back, as it were, upon its own resources; it is what still possesses the last echo of solar forces. Let us keep this moment before us. There were other beings that were more of a plant-like nature, but we will leave these aside at present.

The beings who represented the first material elaboration of the human form at the time of the sun's departure have undergone manifold changes, but in fishes is preserved what reminds us of our separation from the sun; reminds us that at one time we belonged to the sun. The sun departed from the earth and began to influence it from without, and it also influenced the human being on earth. Gradually alternating conditions of consciousness developed—those of waking and sleeping. Gradually the condition developed in which the human being was more united with his I and also with the higher principles (etheric and astral body), in alternation with another condition in which the astral body withdrew from the physical body. This condition is still preserved today in the alternation between waking and sleeping. Let us for a moment consider this alternating condition. We all know it, for it belongs to the most elementary teaching of anthroposophy; we know that when we are awake there is a regular connection between our physical, etheric and astral bodies, and our I. When we are asleep, the astral body and the I withdraw from the physical and etheric body.

In the very early epoch with which we have been dealing the I was not yet present, and in its place part of the etheric body withdrew; this condition may be compared with that of sleep. Now we must clearly understand that we leave the physical and etheric body behind in bed; we really bestow on them a plant-like condition. Plants have a sleep-consciousness, as does our physical and etheric body during sleep. But at the present time, during sleep, the astral body and I of the normal human being also possess a kind of vegetable consciousness, for plant entities too are unaware of their surroundings. This was different in olden times: when the astral body and I withdrew back then, the human being was dimly conscious of the surrounding spiritual world.

We can now form an idea of another important fact which arose through the sun separating from the earth. Before this took place the whole human being, with physical, etheric and astral bodies, was influenced and governed by the material and spiritual sun forces. Subsequently the sun's position was the determining factor for this, depending on whether our physical, etheric and astral bodies were subject to the sun's influence, whether it shone on us directly or not. We may now ask whether, at this epoch, another influence also streamed from the sun. Yes; at the time when no physical eye had as yet seen the sun, when the sun did not as yet penetrate the dense atmosphere of the earth, the human etheric and astral body (when outside the physical body) received important influences from the spiritual forces proceeding from the sun. The human being was unable to perceive these influences, for he was not yet mature enough, but later he became able to do so through receiving a capacity which enabled him to see what streamed spiritually to him from the sun.

What was this event which made the human being capable of perceiving forces indwelling the sun, those sublime powers which had to leave the earth and unite themselves with the sun? When did this perception come to him? Gradually these forces streamed into the earth, and the most important, decisive point of time, when human beings received the capacity to assimilate not only the physical forces, but also the spiritual forces of the sun in full consciousness, was the moment of Christ's coming to the earth.

One might say this therefore: There was a time when the human being separated physically from the sun. Among animals the fish directs our thoughts to this time, for it recalls the human condition before we were obliged to separate from the sun. Then came the time when the higher forces, whose leader is Christ—the great sun spirit—left the earth; after which humankind gradually matured until it was able to receive these higher forces in the same way it could receive physical sun forces from without. Inward spiritual power had to manifest as reality on earth, just as formerly the physical sun forces had manifested. Upon Christ's appearance, it was the task of initiates to remind human beings of their ancient home on the sun, by invoking the symbol of the fish. This is why the fish appears in the catacombs as a true symbol connected with the evolution of humanity; and the pupils of early Christian centuries, seeing the fish symbol everywhere, received the words of the initiates which rang in their ears with deep emotion, for spiritually it led them to the inward holiness of the story of Palestine, and at the same time led them forth cosmically into the mighty evolutionary phases of the earth. Such things as these were studied in the schools of initiation; and in outward symbols such as that of the fish, found in many places, we have an expression of these mysteries, just as geologists see in the fossils of plants tokens of a primeval past. But just as the impress of a fossil points to an original reality, so the symbol of the fish is a token of what was cultivated within the mysteries. This symbol did not appear suddenly. Long before the coming of Christ, prophets of the Messiah had directed their pupils to his coming, and everywhere, back to the time of the Druidic mysteries,[15] the fish symbol played its part in this.

To sum up: there was a time when the moon separated from the earth. Previously the earth and the moon had formed one body. Then the triad of sun, moon, and earth arose. Mighty were the natural catastrophes which then took place; events were of a very tempestuous nature. The physical part of the human being was not then at a very high stage of development, and he left it behind him as an ossified stage of evolution. In order to understand this we must keep one thing in mind: when the sun separated from the earth, the earth went backward in its development; and only after the moon withdrew with the earth's worst constituents did things improve again. There was, therefore, for some time an ascending development until the departure of the sun; then a descending one, when everything became worse, more grotesque; then, after the moon withdrew, a re-ascending evolution again.

From this stage of evolution also, a degenerate form was preserved, one which does not by any means appear now as it did then; but it exists as the form which belonged to humankind before the moon withdrew, before we possessed an I. The animal form which recalls the lowest stage of earthly evolution, the time when the human being plunged most deeply into passions and when the astral body was susceptible to the worst external influences, is that of the serpent, a creature in which is preserved the shameful depths of our evolution on this planet, although what we see now has grown still more degenerate. The symbol of the serpent is also derived from evolution; it is not intellectually conceived but is rooted in the depth of reality. Fish and snake symbols are derived from the mysteries of our evolution. It is quite natural for a person to experience a feeling of pleasure when they see the glistening body of a fish in the pure, chaste watery element; it gives us a feeling of peace, just as, to those of unspoiled sensibility, it gives a feeling of horror to see a creeping snake. Such feelings are certainly not meaningless, but memories of conditions through which we once passed. We like to see the wonderful, living, sun-shimmering form of a fish in water; this recalls our former innocence when we as yet possessed no I, but were governed by the best spirits in evolution. And likewise, upon sight of a slithering snake, we remember the nastiest period in evolution, a time when we came close to lapsing from our evolution altogether. Our feeling experiences of this kind are connected with cosmic realities, a fact that illumines such unconscious experiences of the human soul, seemingly so puzzling but appearing so vividly to those not yet over-cultured. Through such insight many things can become apparent. We can certainly overcome our fear of snakes, but this is something we need to cultivate. The basic feeling of repulsion lives in the soul nevertheless, and it points us back to the ancient times of which I am speaking. They were times when the human being was physically at the snake stage, when those elemental beings set to work of whom we said that they prepared us for freedom, prepared us to receive the Christ in his full meaning and grandeur.

Let us now ask this: Who were the beings who helped prevent us from lapsing, from sinking into the depths? We spoke of them in the previous lecture : they were those who worked on humankind when it had descended to the depths, and who led it again to the heights—the luciferic beings. The sun spirits did not yet work upon humanity; those beings did who sacrificed themselves. They moved amongst the people of the earth in a very remarkable way. Outwardly they had a certain human form, for even the highest spirits have to incarnate in forms which are to be found on earth, so these beings assumed the external shape that was human at that time. In form, they said, we resemble the human being, but our true home is not on the earth; it is upon the two intermediate planets, Venus and Mercury. The best part of their souls were on these planets, but their outward form, which in fact was a kind of illusion, was on earth. They gave humankind what it needed, namely guidance and teaching, for the reason that their home was not on earth, the first planet to be formed, but upon Venus and Mercury. These beings must be described as the first teachers, the first initiates of humanity; outwardly they resembled the human beings of that time, but inwardly they possessed lofty and important qualities enabling them to work upon humanity as a whole, and also to work on the more advanced individuals in special schools, which were the first mystery schools. There were always some of these more advanced individuals who had their home in the stars and who, although connected with the stars, had a human shape and walked amongst humankind.

The human being continued to evolve, and now passed on into the middle of the Atlantean epoch; the present human form only began to develop during the first half of that epoch, and only then did the human being begin to feel fully at home within it. Now, some beings in those ancient times were low down in the scale of humanity. There were others who had preserved their pliability, and again others who only occasionally inhabited human bodies. What I am now about to describe happened very frequently in the first part of the Atlantean epoch. Imagine a human being of that time who, for an Atlantean, was highly evolved; through certain causes it frequently happened that such a human being separated his physical body (which was then very plastic) and his etheric and astral bodies from his more spiritual parts, which then withdrew more into the spiritual world, so as later to take on a different corporeality. It very frequently happened that, long before the physical, etheric and astral bodies were ready to die, their soul and spirit-principles voluntarily departed from them. These bodies, when they had belonged to especially exalted individuals, were pure and good. Highly spiritual beings then allowed themselves to descend into these bodies; and so it frequently happened during the ancient Atlantean epoch that beings who were otherwise unable to incarnate on earth made use of such advanced bodies in order to descend amongst humankind. These were the beings who acted as great teachers in the Atlantean schools of initiation. They worked powerfully with the means available at that time.

When, at that time, the human being left his physical body at night, he had what may be called a dim clairvoyant consciousness. During the day the outline of objects was still indistinct, and there was no such clearly defined difference between the conditions of sleeping and waking as exists today. It happened, therefore, that the ordinary human being beheld such an individual as I have described in an alternating manner—by day perceiving him as a human being, but at night seeing him quite otherwise, in a soul-spiritual way, though knowing it was the same being who appeared to him by day in a physical body. These were beings belonging to Venus and Mercury who intervened in human existence and were with the human being day and night. The memories of these beings remained in the souls who incarnated again and again among the peoples of Europe, and they recalled them when they uttered the names Wotan, Thor and so on. When the inhabitants of Ancient Europe spoke of the gods they were no imaginary figures to them, but memories of forms seen in Atlantis. In the same way, when the Greeks spoke of Zeus, Apollo, and Ares, these were forms they had themselves perceived during the Atlantean epoch. Whereas in the Egyptian age memories of Ancient Lemuria arose, in the Greek age memories of earthly experiences on Atlantis rose within the souls of the people.

We must clearly understand that if everything contained in later religions was a memory of realities connected with former ages of the earth, some very important event would have to occur when the last of these memories had arisen. At roughly the time when the Greeks and Romans recalled the Atlantean epoch, the Christ brought an essentially new impulse into evolution. We indicated the nature of this impulse when we spoke about the long intermediate period of evolution in which luciferic beings were preparing mankind, making it capable of receiving the Christ impulse, so that the sun should not merely send down its external powers, but that inner forces should also stream from it into human beings. This period has not nearly come to an end; it is still in its infancy, for with the coming of Christ only the first impulse was given for the inwardly spiritual part of the sun to stream to earth in addition to physical sunlight. Ever stronger will that light become, which as spiritual sunlight, or Christ-light, will illumine humanity from within in the same way that physical sunlight shines upon us from without. In future we will not only perceive the sun's glories with our outward eyes but will also inwardly experience the sun's spiritual aspect. Only when we can do so will we fully understand what really dwelt on earth as the being whom we call Christ Jesus. Only slowly and gradually will we come to an understanding of this; and just as in pre-Christian times we had to understand the pronouncements of those spiritual beings who guided humankind as it contracted in its descent into the physical world, so by real spiritual effort we must henceforth try to understand the spiritual power which at one time departed from the earth with the sun. We must become able to receive this power again as an inner spiritual force; we must comprehend this Christ power—this spiritual power which imparts to us the great impulse for the future. The object of spiritual science, and of all that can be acquired as spiritual teaching, is to enable us to comprehend this power of Christ. It cannot be said that anthroposophy is Christianity, but we can say that what has been given to humanity and the earth by the Christ principle will be gradually made comprehensible by means of anthroposophy. When that mighty impulse is understood, it will increasingly pour into humanity, for humankind has need of it so that, having sunk most deeply into matter, we may once more wrest ourselves free and return again to our spiritual home.

Lecture 8

STUTTGART, 12 AUGUST 1908

The Human Being's Connection with the Various Planetary Bodies

FOR more exact understanding of our particular subject let us first consider the greater worlds of the cosmos and then look down to the smaller sphere of our immediate earthly existence. We shall be able in this way to form a clear idea of what in spiritual or esoteric science is meant by the three terms we have brought together here—universe, earth and human being.

You will have already gathered from what has been said that in spiritual science one can by no means speak of the world as a merely material entity. We have seen how the various planetary entities (a term I think preferable to planetary bodies) presented here as the different embodiments of our earth—Saturn, Sun and Moon—are something quite different from merely material globes, each being, as we have seen, the dwelling-place of a host of spiritual beings, and created only according to the needs of the spiritual beings that live on them. We saw how the sun separated from the earth because it had to be the home of certain sublime beings who could only make use of the finer substances for their evolution, while the human being had to retain the remaining substances on the earth. Were we to investigate the whole wide universe we should nowhere find anything that is material alone, for everything is connected with a spiritual aspect. We have seen how the various earth beings are connected with spiritual beings. Stones and the minerals of the earth have their I in what surrounds us in the universe. Plants have their I localized in the centre of the earth planet, while their astral principle, which brings about the development of the flower, encircles them above the earth. Everything is pervaded by spirit, and thus our conception of a planetary entity is enlarged. We look up to some heavenly body and we know that it is but the expression of certain spiritual beings connected with a material planet.

Now, by developing certain capacities which are to be found slumbering within us, we can actually gain some knowledge about these planetary entities spread through space; and today we shall consider the human being in relation to the various planets. We are surrounded on earth by minerals, plants, animals and human beings, moreover we know that earthly affairs are regulated by higher beings who in Christian esotericism are described as angels, archangels, and archai. We also know that there are other beings concerned with the earth, even though they send their forces from the sun and the moon. Today we have something to add to this. Let us ask this: To what extent is the nature of a planet in our solar system comparable with any other? To help us here, let us consider the entities that we see visibly before us in the present cycle of humanity, and ask how these entities which surround us here as minerals, plants, animals and human beings relate to other beings in the universe. Of course we are dealing with this question from the standpoint of spiritual science, from knowledge gained through the development of clairvoyant consciousness, something we shall return to later. But in the first place let us ask whether there are on other planets human beings such as those evolving on our earth? Can clairvoyant consciousness discover them? Clairvoyant consciousness does not find humankind on other planets in exactly the same form as upon earth, but we do discover that each planet, each heavenly body, has its particular mission. Nothing in the universe is repeated, other planets have other missions.

Our earth has originated from three preceding embodiments. Other beings previously passed through the stage of existence we are now passing through (the human stage): angels, for example, on Old Moon, archangels on Old Sun, and the spirits of personality or archai upon Old Saturn. It is easy to think, wrongly, that these were at that time human beings like ourselves, but we must bear in mind that on Old Moon no solid stone or mineral existed, and therefore the beings who passed through their human stage there did so under entirely different conditions. Despite this we must still speak of it as the human stage. The archangels or fire spirits passed through their human stage in entirely different conditions, for Old Sun consisted only of warmth and gas, and beings passing through their human evolution there could not possess bodies such as we have, with solid muscles, bones, etc. In earthly evolution nothing is repeated, every stage has its particular mission in the great mansion of cosmic existence.

Let us now turn to the evolution of our earth. Observed esoterically, we see it as a planet inhabited by the human being, where he undergoes evolution. This evolution was only rendered possible because the sun and the moon separated from the earth, so that its forces were held in balance between the two. At the time when the earth was itself still sun (if we may call it so), it passed through an evolution in which it was incorporated with the sun. The sun was then itself at the planetary stage of existence, and was inhabited by archangels, but because of progressive development it was possible for part of what was embodied in it to rise to a higher existence at the cost of that other part which detached itself from the earth as moon. In the great universe, evolution proceeds in such a way that things which for a time have progressed side by side separate, the one expanding into higher regions, the other descending into a lower state. In order that certain beings might be sufficiently ennobled, the sun had itself to become a body fitted for their habitation: it advanced from planetary existence to fixed-star existence. We have to realize that a cosmic entity like our sun has developed from a planet to a sun. In esoteric perception we see how a sun is a planet that has progressed, ascended in evolution.

As was pointed out in the last lecture, after the sun had once more separated at a certain point from the unified cosmic body, the human being continued to dwell for a long period upon the earth without the spiritual sun forces. Then through the advent of Christ the spiritual forces of the sun found again a place upon the earth. Now, if the Christ is incorporated into the earth, humankind must become more and more mature through receiving the Christ principle. The material form of a planet depends on what it evolves in the way of beings. Exactly in the same way as the sun evolved to its present exalted position by withdrawing the finer substances because the entity of the sun had need of them, so this will also be true of the earth. The substances of the earth will have then so changed as to be suited to the human being, or rather to what, in the distant future, will have developed from humankind and from the earth-beings it bears along with it; for when the human being has acquired his full might he will draw other earth beings along with him. What will happen then? If human beings pervade themselves ever more with the Christ principle, if they absorb more and more of the sun forces which descended to earth with the Christ, they will themselves grow ever more Christ-like, and will irradiate the whole earth with the Christ principle.

What is this Christ principle? Before we can know what it is we must know what the mission of the earth is, so that we can use one particular word to describe it. What is the mission of earthly existence? But let us ask first what the mission of Old Moon existence was. If we look back to Old Moon with clairvoyant vision, we find at its beginning, in the ancestors of our present earth beings, a very remarkable quality. These beings possessed a great deal but they lacked one thing at the very beginning of the Old Moon period which we now find everywhere around us on our earth. The forces of the Moon, the predecessor of our earth, worked at first without wisdom; the conditions on the Moon to begin with were such that nowhere could one have perceived wisdom in its harmonious interplay. If one observes the evolution of Old Moon clairvoyantly, one sees how the wisdom of the cosmos was gradually embodied in the beings who dwelt upon Moon by other beings who encompassed it and who worked upon it from without. Because of this, Old Moon is called the planet of wisdom.

When the Moon period came to an end, wisdom was in all things. Life on Moon then passed through an intermediate condition resembling a world-sleep, called 'pralaya', and when the Earth in turn arose from pralaya, its entities brought with them the wisdom with which they had been imbued on Old Moon. The consequence of this is that wisdom is implanted in all we observe around us. In all the entities and creatures resulting from Moon evolution, which have a further mission to fulfil, we find wisdom. Look where you will: take, for example, the leaf of any plant; the more closely you observe it the more wonderful it appears, because its diverse parts are arranged according to the highest wisdom. Take a portion of the human thigh-bone: there also the constituent parts are arranged according to the highest wisdom so as to form a support capable of carrying the upper body. No engineering skill of today can equal the bridge-building of this mighty wisdom. In all the other human organs, and indeed in all the surrounding world, we see wisdom at the root of everything. We human beings must try to incorporate this wisdom into our inner being but can do so at present only in a less than competent way. The wisdom we possess as microcosm is something only to be learnt from the objects that surround us here. Wisdom is in all things, including those aspects of the human being in which we do not consciously participate.

Tracing the course of history, we often extol human wisdom. How wonderful it seems to us when we learn that at a particular moment the human being made this or that discovery. The art of paper making, for example, was discovered as the modern era approached; it was an accomplishment of human intelligence—but wasps knew how to do it long before man. A wasp's nest, however, is not built by individual wasps, but by the group-soul of wasps; it is built of exactly the same material as our paper. These group-souls long ago possessed something which human wisdom will only gain gradually. This wisdom, which is found deeply ingrained in everything that exists on earth, had to take form gradually, and we shall see how this was brought about throughout the Moon period, how at that time wisdom warred with un-wisdom, and how Old Moon then bequeathed to Earth the seeds of entities in whom wisdom had been implanted.

What is to be implanted in a similar way in the beings of our Earth evolution? Just as wisdom was implanted in our predecessors on Old Moon, so love has to be implanted on our planet. Our planet earth is the planet of love. The development of this, the first instilling of love, had to be in its lowest form. This happened during the Lemurian epoch, when the human I coalesced: at that time the development of love in its lowest form began through the separation of the sexes. All further evolution consists in the continual refinement, the spiritualizing, of this love principle. Just as wisdom was instilled into Moon entities during Old Moon, so one day, when our Earth has attained its goal, all earthly beings will be filled with love.

Let us now turn for a moment to the next planetary existence that is to succeed our Earth—the Jupiter embodiment. When the beings reappear who will inhabit Jupiter, they will regard all those in their environment with their own spiritual powers of perception. And just as with our intellect we admire the wisdom contained in stones, plants, and animals, and indeed in everything that surrounds us—just as we draw wisdom from them so that we also may possess it—so Jupiter beings will direct their forces to all that surrounds them, and the love which was implanted in them during Earth evolution will pass like fragrance to those who now surround them. In the same way that we analyse objects and learn from the wisdom contained in them, so the Jupiter beings will edify themselves with the outpourings of love that proceed from the beings surrounding them. This love which is to develop on Earth can only develop through earthly I's encountering one another in the way described. Evolution toward this can only occur by virtue of human beings having been sundered from group-soul qualities and drawing close to one another again as separate beings. Only thus can true love develop. Where I's are united within the group-soul there is no true love. Beings must be separated from each other so that love may be offered as a free gift. Only by such a separation as has come about in the human kingdom, where I meets I as independent individual, has love as a free gift become possible. This is why an increasing individualism and a reuniting of separate individuals had to come about on earth.

Think of the various beings united within a group-soul; the group-soul directs them as to how they shall act. Can it be said that the heart loves the stomach? No, the heart is united with the stomach by the being within who render them a unity. In the same way the diverse animals in a group are united one with the other within their group-soul nature, and what they have to do is governed by the wise group-soul. Only when this group-nature is overcome, and individual confronts individual, can the sympathy of love be offered as a free gift from one being to another. Human beings could only be prepared for this mission gradually, and we see how they pass through a kind of preparatory school for love before they become fully individualized. We see how, before they wholly possessed an I of their own, guiding beings gathered them into groups related by blood, and the members of these groups loved each other because of the blood tie. This was a time of great preparation for humanity. We have already pointed out that at this stage love was not a free gift, but was governed by a remnant of cosmic wisdom. We have seen how luciferic beings worked here and, with their strong liberating force, opposed everything that gathered humankind into families and peoples through the power of the blood. These luciferic beings strove to make the human being independent. Thus humankind continued gradually to mature so that it might eventually receive the highest power of love—the Christ principle, which expressed its nature in the words, 'He who does not forsake father, mother, son, and daughter, he who does not take up his cross and follow me, is not worthy of me.'[16] These words are not to be understood trivially, but in the sense that, through reception of the Christ principle, the ancient blood brotherhood had to assume a new form, a feeling of 'belonging to each other' which, regardless of material foundations, must pass from soul to soul, from person to person. The Christ principle has given the impulse by which one person can love another, and through this Christianization it will be possible for human love to become more and more spiritual. Love will become more soulful and more spiritual, and by virtue of this humankind will also draw along with it the lower creatures, and will thus transform the earth. In a far distant future humankind will transform the entire substance of the earth, and bring the earth-body to maturity so that it can at last reunite with the sun. Christ as spiritual sun has given the impulse by which the earth and the sun can again be united in one body at a future time.

We have surveyed the course of the evolution of the world and have seen how the body of the sun first separated from the earth, and how the mighty Christ impulse descended, bringing the impulse for a reunion of earth and sun to make possible an ascent to higher stages of existence. We have also seen that the earth is to produce human beings who have this as their mission. Therefore, when we look around us at the human kingdom, and desire to learn about humankind, we can find it only on the earth, for only here are conditions produced for such human beings as exist today. You may now ask how is it with the other kingdoms of the earth? Let us consider the plant kingdom. When clairvoyant vision sweeps out into the universe and we investigate the other planets belonging to our system, we find in all those belonging to our sun a plant kingdom entirely corresponding to our own—so that in our plant kingdom we have something whose systematic life, as we may call it, is a part of our whole universe. Our solar system is populated by plant entities, and were the whole matter to be considered esoterically we should see that each planet is peopled also by its own kind of human beings. It is easy to perceive an inner relationship between plants and the sun, and how the life of the plant is intimately connected with the life of the sun. If this is the case it must also be connected with all the planets belonging to the solar system. When we allow our thoughts to sweep back to the condition of the earth when it was still Sun, we find that the human being consisted of physical and etheric body, that is, he was at the stage of a plant. The human being at that time had the qualities of a plant; he was of a kind which the vegetable kingdom now embodies. This plant kingdom is composed of entities consisting of physical body and etheric body. Observing them, we say that they have remained true to the sun: they still clearly reveal their relationship with the sun.

Let us consider the nature of a plant according to Rosicrucian wisdom. We see the plant fixed in the ground by its roots, that is, the organ which leads it towards the centre of the earth—to its I; and we see how it turns its organs of reproduction to the sun and absorbs its chaste rays. Then let us turn to the human being. It is not difficult to imagine the human being as an inverted plant. If we think of a plant exactly inverted, we have the human being, with reproductive organs turned to the centre of the earth, and root towards the cosmos. The animal stands half-way between these. Hence one can say in a spiritual sense that when the soul-nature of the world passed through the various kingdoms it passed through a plant, an animal, and a human existence. Plato expresses this in a beautiful way.

He says: 'The world-soul is crucified on the cross of the world body.'[17] The human being has passed through the plant stage which directed him to the centre of the earth. The position of animals is expressed in the horizontal position of the spine. The human being's stance is that of the plant reversed. Thus the cross arose.

On it the world soul is crucified; this is the profound esoteric meaning of the cross. In the plant of today we have an entity which strives towards the sun, which has, in a certain sense, remained united with the sun, hence it has the opposite direction from the human being. Animal forms on the various planetary embodiments are partly alike and partly different; here too the animal stands midway between the human being and plant. If we now pass to the mineral kingdom we find in the forms of crystals something that directs us into the cosmos far beyond our solar system. In the formative forces of the mineral kingdom we find forces which reach far beyond the solar system. We are led, especially when considering translucent forms of the mineral kingdom, to a perception of what takes place far beyond our solar system. The mineral is most generalized in nature, has least individual existence, yet forms at present the foundation of our life. It has a universal existence. The higher the entity, the more it is suited to the solar system of our earth and sun.

But now let us consider the same question in relation to humankind. If human beings were adapted to forces that ruled on the earth alone they would be condemned to exist only on the earth: they could never become citizens of the universe and could speak of nothing that takes place beyond the earth. Though they are indeed adapted in their outward form to earthly conditions, through their higher powers they also join with all the higher beings who are connected with the earth. What limits us as human beings to the earth relates to our body alone; the spiritual powers with which we are furnished lead us far beyond the earth. Here again we have to distinguish between different forces. In order that we may understand them let us dwell first on those forces that can be easily classified. We have in the first place the power which called up pictures before our spiritual eyes during the Atlantean epoch. Human consciousness, to begin with, was a picture consciousness; only as evolution progressed did we gradually become able to comprehend external objects by means of our object consciousness. The consciousness which at the present time presents the sense world to us so that we see colours with our eyes, hear sounds with our ears, smell, and taste, was originally undifferentiated and at a certain point emerged from the general perception of warmth mediated by the organ which was then like a kind of lantern in us—the pineal gland. Object consciousness is purely of the earth. Wonderful as it may seem, all the sensations that we are aware of as human beings, such as the colour of objects, resonant tones, only exist on earth; and if we were to observe the beings of another planet we would find that we would not initially understand them. For instance, if we were to say something to these beings about the colour red they would not know what was meant; on their planet they have a different way of perceiving beings and things. What we call sense-perception applies only to our particular planet.

I have already explained that before sense-perception was differentiated it was inwardly connected with reproduction. Precisely as sense-perception is of the earth, so also is the form of earthly reproduction (as it exists at present) adapted to this planetary existence: it exists for the purpose of providing the first foundation of what is the mission of the earth, namely, love—for love is to be developed upon the earth.

We now come to another human power. Suppose you observe some object: as long as your eyes are turned to it you know that you are in correspondence with the object—it acts upon you. Now turn your eyes away and hold the idea-picture of it in your memory: the object has gone but the image remains. If human beings did not have the capacity of retaining such images they would be beings of an entirely different kind, for as soon as our gaze turned away from the object in question, the image of it would also have disappeared, and in consequence we would be unable to connect the attributes of the things observed with our own attributes. That capacity of consciousness which today enables us to retain the image of an object even when the object itself is gone, was ours even on Old Moon: it is the same capacity which then enabled us to see what was external to us in pictures. We could not at that time see outer objects as we do today, but when anything approached us an astral vision rose before us like a vivid dream-picture, yet one that related in a particular way to the object we perceived. Human consciousness was then a picture consciousness, not an object consciousness. Now we relate to objects themselves, the picture we see is that of the object. A last remnant of picture consciousness has remained in our power to form memory pictures. These are of greater value than the mere observation of external objects. In observing a number of objects that are similar to each other we bring them together in one general idea. For instance, you have here so many pieces of chalk and you group them under the general conception 'chalk'. In this way the human being rises to general conceptions for which no outer object exists. As human beings we can work inwardly with our ideas, and if with this inward activity—with this power of ideation—we were to come into relation with beings outside our planetary existence, we would be able, without having to refer to any object, to make ourselves more easily understood by them. Both the picture consciousness (which human beings possessed as a dim clairvoyance before they could perceive outer objects) and also the imaginative consciousness which they will subsequently develop, are more comprehensive than mere sense observation.

When picture consciousness is acquired through esoteric development and you are able to perceive not only outer objects, but also, for instance the human aura, when in pictures you see around you things of a soul and spirit nature, when what exists in the world rises before you in pictorial symbols, you have gained with imaginative consciousness the power to connect with other beings inhabiting the planetary world.

There is a yet higher degree of consciousness. Humankind dimly possessed this during Sun evolution, and still possesses it faintly during sleep—it is dreamless sleep consciousness. People are not devoid of consciousness when asleep in the same way that a plant is not without consciousness; plant consciousness is the same as that of the human being in ordinary sleep. Sleep is only a lower degree of consciousness, when things escape the human being's attention and he does not observe them. Through developing certain capacities we can gain the power to perceive what is around us in the state of dreamless sleep. This is a higher state of consciousness than picture consciousness; it is the consciousness plants have, but in a sleeping form. If one rises to this consciousness but pervades it with one's I in clear day-consciousness, one has attained in esoteric development to the level of Inspiration or inspired consciousness. This consciousness is not one of pictures merely. When what flows from things passes into the observer it is a sounding, resounding consciousness, and cannot be compared with picture consciousness. The person who experiences it enters into a spiritual world of tone—the consciousness described by Pythagoras[18] as 'the Harmony of the Spheres'. The whole world then utters forth its nature, and when we are asleep at night and the astral body and I are withdrawn from the physical and etheric bodies, the harmonies and melodies of cosmic music pervade our astral body. The astral body is then immersed in true spiritual existence, and from the music of the spheres it draws power by which to restore its depleted forces. At night we are plunged in the music of the spheres, and through the tones ringing within us we feel strengthened and refreshed when morning comes. When conscious of this, we are inspired, and are capable of perceiving all that is contained within the solar system.

Through the ordinary senses and the intellect associated with them, we perceive only the things of the earth; through Imagination we come into connection with the diverse planets; and when we have attained Inspiration we enter into connection with the solar system. This fact has always been known in certain circles. Goethe, who was an initiate, knew it; hence in the prologue to *Faust*, set in the spiritual world in heaven, he represents the angel as saying:

> The sun intones his ancient song,
> 'Mid rival chant of brother spheres.

From this we see that he knew that the secrets of the solar system are expressed in tones, and that one who can raise himself to Inspiration can learn these secrets. Goethe did not write this by chance, as we can see, for he maintains the theme. In the *Faust* Part II, when he takes the protagonist up into the spiritual world, he says again very much the same thing:

> Sounding loud to spirit ears,
> Lo! the new-born day appears.

Spirit ears are the ears of the clairvoyant, who is able to perceive the harmonies of the solar system. If you could perceive the sun forces streaming down on to the bodies of plants as they grow, these bodies whose roots and leaves culminate in flowers around which the astral body streams, and into which flow the forces of the sun—if you could perceive these forces mysteriously entering through the flower, you would perceive them as spiritual music, the music of the spheres. This can, however, only be heard by spiritual ears. Spiritual sound enters into flowers, that is the secret of the growth of plants: each separate flower is the expression of the tones which give it form, and endow the fruit with its character. The plant receives sun tones which hold sway within it as spirit. You perhaps know how form can be imparted by sound in the material world; you may remember the experiment of the Chladni sound patterns:[19] how sand scattered upon a disc acquires certain figures as the result of sound. In these forms and patterns we have the expression of the sound that produces them. Just as physical sound is captured, as it were, in this sand, so the spiritual sound of the sun is captured and absorbed by flower and fruit. It is concealed mysteriously in the seed, and when a new plant grows from the seed, the sun-tone it has absorbed conjures forth the form of the plant again.

Clairvoyant consciousness looks upon the plant kingdom, seeing everywhere in the flowers which form the variegated tapestry of the earth's surface the reflection of sun-tones. What Goethe says is true, 'The sun intones his ancient song', but it is also true that these sun-tones stream to earth, are absorbed by plants, and reappear when new plants spring from the seed. For in the forms of plants the sun-tones, the echoes of the music of the spheres, reverberate into physical space. Here we see how universe and earth, how fixed star and planet, are inwardly, spiritually connected, and we learn not only to look at what is in our environment in the physical world, but we also gain an inkling of how those who partake of Inspiration ascend to the sun.

There is a still higher state of consciousness, which we call Intuition in its true sense: by means of this the human being can slip into the very nature of things. This is more than inspirational consciousness; here a person, as it were, plunges into other beings, unites with them. This leads us still further. Where does inspirational consciousness lead us? It leads us to where we feel one with the earth, for the I's of the plants are at the centre of the earth. When we encompass the sun's resounding tone we become one with the planetary being that dwells at the centre of the earth; we become one with his planet and can also become one with all other beings. We then have experiences that reach far beyond our solar system; our vision is extended from solar-system consciousness to cosmic consciousness. Intuition carries us beyond the various solar systems.

Thus we see that in the mineral kingdom we have something whose homogeneous form furnishes us with a foundation that extends far beyond our ordinary existence. We see that the present human form is a physical earthly form, but that humankind raises itself once more from ordinary earthly consciousness to planetary consciousness through Imagination; to solar system consciousness through Inspiration; to cosmic consciousness through Intuition. This is the path humanity has to travel in so far as it is connected with the entire evolution of the world. In the next lecture we shall descend from these heights, having studied what has unfolded in more recent ages of earthly existence, in the Egyptian and Greek ages, and in our own age, to see how the greater macrocosm, the mighty universe of which we have formed some idea today, is reflected in the life and conception of the individual human being, the microcosm.

Lecture 9

STUTTGART, 13 AUGUST 1908

Conquest of the Physical Plane in Post-Atlantean Civilizations

OUR task now is to comprehend the spiritual horizon within which we stand today by investigating the human being's origins. We have seen that in the course of human evolution through the Lemurian and Atlantean epochs humankind has gradually acquired its present form. We will now extend our study of this second epoch, the Atlantean, on into our own era so far as is necessary for an understanding of our subject.

We know that prior to the middle of the Atlantean epoch human consciousness was quite different to what it is today. While in the physical body during the day, people then by no means saw objects with the same sharp outlines they do now: everything was more or less blurry. And when at night they left their physical body, they did not sink into dreamless sleep, but were able to perceive spiritual beings in a world of spirit. Let us pass over the fact that these beings (who also sought embodiment in Atlantean bodies) entered into a certain companionship with man, instead only reminding ourselves that at that time people had the conviction, based on direct experience, that above the human kingdom to which they themselves belonged there were other kingdoms—that of the angels and of the archangels—and that they learned to recognize these higher beings spiritually face to face, just as we now learn to recognize each other in the physical world. Then came the time when waking object consciousness became ever clearer, and, on the other hand, when dimness and darkness enveloped the human being at night. This was the period when the first rudimentary germs of the I or 'I am' were implanted into the human being. By learning to perceive the objects around him, at the same time he gained that form of self-awareness that he was intended to develop.

We must conceive of everything in the world in terms of degree. Just as there are all possible levels of beings in the animal and human kingdoms so also there are many different levels of beings above humankind. Some beings in the kingdom of the angels are very close to the human level, and others are at a higher stage; we find many levels and degrees when we direct our gaze to the higher worlds. We have in the first place to understand clearly that at the time when people rose at night through dim clairvoyant consciousness into higher worlds, these beings also gained something (to put it trivially) through dialogue with human beings: their own being was enriched. Though these beings stood higher than the human being, they were still inwardly connected with him; they inspired him and influenced his imaginative consciousness, which was, however, dim. So that we must think of the human being in that ancient period as being in a condition in which, when he withdrew from his physical and etheric bodies, a higher being, or, in a wider sense, a whole host of higher beings, as it were, received him. Fundamentally this is also the case today, only people now are unaware of it, whereas at that time they were aware, though in a dim clairvoyant way. It has already been mentioned in other lectures that sleep is by no means unnecessary for us; it serves a very great purpose. During the day we continually deplete our physical and etheric bodies. The life we lead from morning till evening exhausts these bodies, and what we feel as fatigue is nothing more than the expression of the fact that within our physical and etheric bodies, indirectly through the astral body, all kinds of sense-perceptions have been taking place in us as well as impulses of joy, of sorrow, and of pain; all these have been playing through us. This wears out our physical and etheric bodies, and in the evening we are tired because all day long we have been wearing them out. At night, when we leave these bodies on the bed, the astral body and I are not inactive: all night long they send their forces into the physical and etheric bodies, working to repair the depleted and worn-out forces of these bodies. They could not do this if, as they withdrew, they were not taken up into a higher kingdom. Above the human kingdom a spiritual kingdom extends, the kingdom of the angels, archangels and other beings. It is like an ocean of spirits surrounding us, from whom we are separated during the day because our perceptions are enclosed within the shell of our bodies. At night we plunge into this spiritual ocean, and from it our astral body absorbs forces which it then pours into the physical and etheric bodies to repair them. Nowadays people are unconscious of this, but at the time when they still possessed dim clairvoyant consciousness they saw how their astral body and I separated from the other members and were absorbed into the divine world of spirit.

Things seen in one way in the physical world have a very different appearance above. One might even say that the gods benefit by thus participating in humanity. In order rightly to understand the relationship of the human being to the universe we must try to form a conception that is not so easy but is necessary if we are to understand our true relationship with the world. We have said that the earth is the planet of love, that love will be truly developed only upon the earth. It is bred or developed here; and by participating in humankind the gods will also come to know love, though in another sense it is they who bestow it. It is difficult to picture this. It is entirely possible for one being to impart a gift to another yet only come to know this gift *through* the other. Picture to yourselves an exceedingly rich person who has never known anything but riches, nor ever experienced the deep satisfaction of soul which results from charity. Picture this person now as doing something good: they give to the poor. The gift calls forth great thankfulness in the soul of the needy individual and this feeling of gratitude is at the same time a gift: it would never have come about if a rich person had not first given. They engender the feeling of gratitude, although they do not feel it themselves, and are only acquainted with it through its reflection, which streams back to them from the person in whom they roused it. It is approximately in this way that the gift of love is imparted to the human being by the gods. They have progressed so far that they are able to kindle love in human beings, who thus become able to learn and acquire it; but the gods only learn to know it as a reality through humankind.

From their heights the gods reach down into the ocean of humanity and feel the warmth of love. We know that the gods lack something when the human being does not live in love. The more human love there is on earth the more food for the gods there is in heaven; the less love there is, the more the gods go hungry. The offering of humankind to the gods is nothing other than the love engendered in human beings that streams up to them.

It is not difficult to picture that in ancient times, when people were still conscious of the divine, this reciprocity—this mutual giving, from human beings and from the gods—was quite different to what it became later. Indeed, because the human being could no longer rise by means of dim clairvoyant consciousness, there were some among the divine spiritual beings who could no longer descend, or reach the sphere of humanity. Throughout the Atlantean epoch, the human being lived with numerous divine beings, and the less capable he became of looking up to the gods the less could a certain category of divine beings experience all they had formerly been able to experience through him. When Atlantis came to an end there were among the Atlantean gods some who suffered hunger, if we may so express it, because they could no longer find the way to humankind.

We must now picture the further evolution of the human being from this perspective. We know that there was a land in the neighbourhood of Ireland where dwelt the most advanced beings of the Atlantean epoch, those who were best prepared to pass through advanced development. These now journeyed from the West to the East, populating Europe, where some remained at a particular stage of evolution, while others went further. The most advanced passed on to the neighbourhood of Central Asia, others into Africa. There were already in these parts some people left over from the older Lemurian and Atlantean epochs; these now mixed in diverse ways, and from them arose the people whom the Greeks represent in many artistic forms as the types of Satyr, Hermes and Zeus. In this migration from West to East we must picture how human consciousness increasingly changed. Those who had come over from Atlantis still possessed a remnant of ancient clairvoyant consciousness, but this continually diminished. At the time of the Atlantean catastrophe there were some even among those who had journeyed towards Asia, Europe and Africa who had already lost every trace of clairvoyance, and others again who still had some remnants of it.

Everywhere under certain conditions there were some who (between sleeping and waking, for example) were able to obtain a clear view into the spiritual worlds. The spiritual being known as Wotan, for instance, was a 'personality' well known to the Atlanteans; we might say that all the ancient Atlanteans were more or less in close touch with him, as some people today form a connection with a monarch, but this conscious connection was gradually lost. Among the peoples of Europe, especially the ancient Germans, there were many who, in an intermediate condition between sleeping and waking, could enter into relationship with Wotan, who actually existed in the spiritual world. Yet owing to the advance in evolution he was constrained and could no longer make himself so generally known as before. There were people in Asia also who knew him, and this knowledge continued on into later times to which even history refers, a time when there was an original natural clairvoyance, and people could speak of the gods from their own experience.

We must keep before us the fact that the human being increasingly descended into the material world, and that because of this the gods were less and less able to maintain their connection with him. Many of the gods were able only to have companionship with certain outstanding human beings. Certain of the gods were unable to descend to ordinary humanity, but could only make contact with individuals who rose to meet them, who advanced in development toward their level. The varied dispositions of human beings, and the remnants of old clairvoyance, as well as the principle of initiation, mingled in a strange way, and this intermingling was preserved in the consciousness of the Teutonic peoples.

During the Atlantean epoch people knew that during sleep, when outside the physical and etheric bodies, they rose into the kingdom of the gods: the gods were known to them, and they knew they would meet them there again. It was felt as a kind of punishment when, after death, human beings were for a time unable to behold the gods and to be received into their company—when, after death, they had to pass through a period of probation because of having become too entangled in material existence. Among those in a position to value material life less than non-material life, the conviction grew that they were not bound to the material world, but that immediately after death they could enter the kingdom of the spirit, which was well known to them. The opinion was held by the various peoples inhabiting Europe that those men who fought bravely and met death on the field of battle, who valued the honours of war more highly than material honours, were not dependent on material existence. They were convinced that in such a case the hero met with some deity or other immediately after death. Those who did not die on the battlefield, who had not learnt to value spiritual possessions more than material life, were said to have died ignobly, and not to be mature enough to be taken immediately into the realm of the spirit, but would first have to enter a kingdom in which they would have to undergo certain trials.

This idea is expressed in the meeting with the Valkyries, and is connected with an ancient clairvoyant memory. It was rightly thought that the human being who met death on the field of battle was taken up by the Valkyries; and it fully accords with such an outlook that in Europe this developed into initiation symbolism. Among other peoples other ideas had developed, but in Europe personal bravery and personal excellence were considered to be most valuable. Initiation was always rightly regarded as something through which someone can already experience during life what they normally only experienced after death, that is, direct communication with the spiritual world. In the same way that the warrior only encountered the Valkyries upon the battlefield, it was apparent that those who sought initiation had to experience this in physical life. In one part of Europe, Siegfried[20] was seen as the last of the initiation heroes. This is preserved in the legend of Siegfried, which tells how the hero united himself with the Valkyries during life, just as dying warriors did upon the battlefield.

Let us now try to enter into the mentality of those who migrated from the West towards the East. They had risen in a certain way to a point where they were fit to enter upon a further development. They had not become ossified, and had within them the rudiments of a more perfect development, but they had retained a comparatively strong clairvoyant capacity. Among all the people who had departed from Atlantis the Europeans were most gifted with clairvoyance; it was less strong among those who peopled Africa. Those who had emigrated earlier into Asia, and who were among the most advanced, came upon a still older people who were in possession of a still older clairvoyance, so that there was much clairvoyance in those parts. Then there was a certain small colony of the most advanced people of the Atlantean epoch who had settled near the Gobi Desert. What kind of people were these, and what do we mean when we say they were the 'most advanced'? It means those *least* able to see into the spiritual world, for advancement consisted in their having proceeded from the spiritual world and having entered the physical world. They were the people who felt constrained to say: 'Formerly we had connection with the spiritual world, but we have it no longer.' This loss filled their hearts with sorrow; they longed for the spiritual world from which they had come and which they valued more than that in which they now dwelt.

Conditions varied among the different European populations. Under certain conditions many could still see into the spiritual worlds. When the mysteries still existed in Europe, and initiates—who through esoteric development could rise in full consciousness to the spiritual world—spoke of those worlds and of the beings dwelling there, or of the varied roles that human souls had to play after death, bringing all this in mighty pictures before the people in the forms of myth and legend, they found some who understood them, for some still had a degree of vision of such things. The distinctive conditions and mode of life in Ancient Europe caused even uninitiated people to experience the spiritual world. Though they could not come into contact with the higher gods they believed in the spiritual worlds and trusted in them. These worlds were real to them, hence they felt their humanity in a quite different way from other peoples. Let us try to enter into the feelings of these ancient Europeans who felt they were indeed connected with the gods. Through consciousness of this a strong sense of personality developed in them, a special sense of the divine worth of the human personality, and above all a strong sense of freedom. We must picture this state of feeling vividly, for it was this consciousness of personality which the people of Europe took with them when they went south and peopled the Greek and Italian peninsulas. Especially we can discern remnants of this feeling among the ancient Etruscans. Even in their art we can observe this strong sense of freedom, for it had a spiritual foundation. Before the rise of the Roman Empire there was an Etruscan population in the Italian peninsula which had a high degree of freedom in its system of government; on one hand it was somewhat hierarchical, and, on the other, free in the highest sense. Each town ensured and defended its own freedom, and an ancient Etruscan would have felt any kind of federal system, in our sense of the word, as unbearable. Everything which migrated southwards in the peninsula as a sense of freedom, or a feeling for personality, sprang from the causes we have mentioned.

Those others who had gone far into Asia included a small company from whom the divine spiritual world had withdrawn the furthest. In its place they had acquired something else, something that had been saved from the world which had withdrawn into profoundest darkness—this was the I, or 'I am'. They felt that what was preserved within them as the 'I am' was the eternal core of their being, and that it had sprung from the spiritual world; they felt all the forms they had previously seen were like a sacred memory, and that their strength depended upon this firm core which remained within them. As yet they did not perceive the I in its complete form; this only came later, but those who were the most advanced, who had descended most deeply, developed a certain tendency which they might have expressed as follows: What we have to treasure above all else is the consciousness of our divinity, consciousness of something in which is to be found the deepest memories of our soul. Even if this soul has forgotten the divine beings which once it knew, we can find the way back to them by looking within our own being—by being conscious of our I. In short, the consciousness of a formless god was now elaborated, a god who does not appear in outward form, but who must be sought within a person's innermost being. This conception, which is a very ancient one, was transformed in the course of human evolution into the commandment: Thou shalt not make to thyself any graven image or likeness of thy God.

In primeval ages the human being experienced God through an image. Now the image had withdrawn into the invisible world, and people strove with all strength to draw a conception of God from their own I: there, where God is formless, the human being sought to form a conception of him through thinking, and to feel his potency. This was not immediately possible. During the first post-Atlantean civilization the memory of what had been lost was still too vivid. In their souls people felt, 'The door is shut,' and the longing to enter again into the spiritual world was too strong. Hence in the first age of civilization the people were filled with longing for the hidden world of the spirit; they looked up with great reverence to the initiates and besought them to grant them entry again to this lost world. And under the influence of the initiates, the first great age of post-Atlantean culture was founded through colonization. This was the wonderful, awe-inspiring pre-Vedic culture, the last remnants of which are to be found in the Vedas; in it the longing for the spiritual world was so great that people strove by artificial means to regain contact with the spirits and gods which they had lost. The longing to fly from the physical world into which they had entered was overwhelmingly strong; we find this feeling in the souls of those who were instructed by the initiates—the holy rishis. We see developing in them a feeling which they might have expressed as follows: 'The world of the physical plane into which we have now entered, which we see spread out around us, is merely illusion: it is worthless, it is maya; but the world lying behind this illusory physical plane is valuable.' Thus a feeling of the worthlessness of the physical plane developed, a feeling of the need to flee from it in order to attain what was spiritual. A feeling evolved which was the basis of this ancient civilization: that human beings must lose their strong sense of personality if they were to be conscious of their divine origin. They strove for complete absorption in the divine, with extinction of the personality: this was of more value to them than life within the personality. We must try to understand the mood of this ancient civilization, and then we shall understand this turning away from all that was material, and how, if someone desired to seek the divine they had to free themselves from sensory bondage and dispel all illusion, escape from maya.

Such was the nature of the first post-Atlantean age; but the mission of all post-Atlantean culture is that human beings should make the surroundings in which they dwell ever more their own, mastering them more and more. In the Persian, that is, the pre-Zarathustran civilization, we see the first phase of the conquest of the external world. The ancient Persians (we refer here to the prehistoric Persians arising from a colony of the last migrating Atlanteans) had already a different consciousness from that of the ancient Indians; they regarded the physical plane as something real. It no longer appeared strange to them; they said: 'We can bring spirit into the physical plane and can cultivate it here.' They paid attention to the physical plane; they did not study it as yet, but they respected it: the ancient Persians still perceived a hostile element in their surroundings, but thought that the enemy could be overcome. The Persians made a friend and companion of the god Ormuzd in order to redeem matter. They worked into the physical world gradually, beginning to perceive that this is not only maya, not merely soulless appearance, but a reality that must be taken into account.

In the great migration towards the East there was another group which moved more towards Asia Minor and Africa, where the Chaldean and Egyptian civilizations were founded. Through them a further step forward was made in the conquest of the physical plane. Here the condition of the people was such that they no longer regarded sense reality as merely hostile or illusory. When they looked up to the stars they said: 'Those stars are not maya, they are not mere appearances!' They thought much about the stars, and studied how one star approached another and what changes took place in the constellations. They felt the stars were an outward expression of the ruling gods, a script which the gods had written: what they saw was not merely appearance but a revelation of the gods. Thus a further step is taken: sense-perceptible matter was now considered as an expression of the deity. The human being thus began to look for wisdom in sensory things. In the Egyptian world the human gaze was turned from the heavens and directed to the earth: geometry was studied so that the earth might be measured. That to which the spirit could attain was thus joined with substance perceived by the senses—an essential advance in evolution. Thus, step by step, evolution progressed.

Now, within the third cultural epoch a small company formed which separated off in a certain way and absorbed all that could be gained from ancient tradition as well as from recent knowledge. This small company, whose initiates had preserved the ancient wisdom and the earlier companionship with the gods, knew how to impart what they had gained as experience from the spiritual world, and they had also absorbed the wisdom of the Chaldeans—the inscriptions of the gods in the cosmos—as well as the wisdom of Egypt, which expressed the union of spirit with what is physical. This group of people, who in a certain sense may be called the 'chosen people', had to make preparation for the greatest period in the world's history. These are the people of the Old Testament, whose Scriptures were the greatest and most significant document of long-past events and also of those that were to come. It is not only an academic error but farcical to suppose that any other Creation story comes anywhere near the Old Testament in value, for it portrays in mighty pictures man's descent from divine heights, and shows at the same time how historical experiences are connected with cosmic events. All this is contained in the Old Testament, and, above all, its contents correspond exactly with the realities of evolution.

And so we have now seen how the rudimentary germ of the human I was prepared step by step in earthly evolution. We have seen that this rudimentary germ would never have been able to evolve if the sun, and afterwards the moon, had not separated from the earth. It was only possible for it to develop through the gradual circumscribing and eventual loss of the human being's vision of the spiritual world. Let us consider how this rudimentary germ developed. What had the human being gradually learnt during the earth's evolution? We must first look back to those ancient times when humankind was as yet unable to see physically, but dwelt in the spiritual world; then came the time when the external objects of the physical world appeared to us as if blurred, when we could still also perceive the spiritual world as well. Who prepared human beings so that in later times, when they were to behold the sun clearly, they should be ready for this change? It was the God we call Jehovah who brought the human being to full maturity. It was he who separated himself from the Elohim so that, from the moon, he could prepare for the most important moment in the earth's evolution. While the human being was still unable to see the external world, Jehovah instilled I-consciousness into him. It was he who, at the time of the old dim clairvoyant consciousness, entered the human being at initiation; and it was he who appeared to the human being in dreams and prepared him slowly to receive the I which he could obtain fully only through the coming of Christ.

Christ did not come, or descend, all of a sudden, but in Jesus Christ made his final, personal appearance. In ancient times he worked also through the Prophets. Christ himself indicates this in the Gospel of John, where he says that those who did not believe Moses and the Prophets would not believe him either, for Moses and the Prophets spoke of him, not indeed as already on earth, but as one whom they foretold. In this sense Christ has a certain prior history in earthly evolution. If we go back to the ancient mysteries we find everywhere the story of Christ and his descent. Let us for a moment consider the European mysteries. We find in all of them a certain tragic feature. If one transports oneself back into these ancient mysteries, one always finds that the teachers told their pupils: 'You may raise yourselves to divine heights, and receive a high degree of initiation, but there is something you cannot yet know fully, something for which you must wait and which we can only indicate: this is the coming of Christ.'

They always spoke of Christ in the northern mysteries as 'He who would come'; they knew him everywhere, but not as one already on the earth. The initiates in Asia and Egypt also knew him as the approaching Christ. 'One day,' they said, 'he will appear.' They knew also that the ancient mysteries could not lead human beings to the highest stage of development. This idea has been preserved symbolically, though we must not over-define such things; they must be conceived subtly, partly as truth and partly as allegory, and not be outlined too sharply. Some echo of this tragic feature regarding the ancient gods and the waiting for the Christ has survived. The glory of the old gods was to fade before the glory of Christ. This is found even in late legends of the Teutonic gods, where something remarkable is ascribed to Siegfried—he was seen as invulnerable, in the sense of the European mysteries, as having the strength of an initiate; however, he possessed one vulnerable place, where he was wounded and thus met his death. In what place was he vulnerable? The place on which later the cross was laid on the one whom they awaited with such expectation. The place where Siegfried was vulnerable was covered by the cross on the stations of the journey to Golgotha. This legend contains a last memory of that tragic feature which informs all the ancient European Mysteries. But in those other mysteries into which Moses was initiated, from which the Old Testament proceeded, and which Moses implanted in his people so far as seemed possible to him, this strange feature in human evolution is often referred to. It is more than a mere picture; there is something which imparts deep reality to it, which we might illustrate as follows. Let us think of the fourfold human being—astral body and I, etheric and physical bodies—as being shone upon by the sun. Through Christ's coming to the earth, the human being has become able to absorb both the physical *and* spiritual forces of the sun. Previously this was different. Then, during sleep, when at night the astral body and I were outside the physical body and etheric body, direct sunlight did not fall upon the human being, only sunlight that was reflected from the moon. The human being absorbed this reflected light, not the direct sunlight. This is exactly the same (in an external, symbolic, yet true form) as in the case of the Christ, who lived as the spiritual aspect of sunlight, and Jehovah, who reflected the true Christ-light until such time as humankind was sufficiently mature to receive it directly. Jehovah sent the Christ down to humanity as if from a mirror. Human beings were speaking of him when they spoke of Jehovah. Hence Jehovah says to Moses: 'Say to thy people, I am the "I AM".' This was the name later given to the Christ. He would not as yet turn his own countenance to humankind. Jehovah prepared humanity, sending them the image of Christ before Christ himself descended, for human beings first had to learn to comprehend the complete descent of Christ into the physical world with his 'I am' into the depths of their own being. Therefore this people, which had been prepared in the truest sense for the coming of Christ, held most firmly to the conception of a formless God. They had to attain to a new conception of God, not merely to remember an old form. This people with its Jehovah religion became in fact those who prepared for the coming of the Christ.

Now, we must clearly understand that everything that has to be specially striven for in the world must proceed from strong impulses. Hence the idea of the power of the formless God informed the whole of the Old Testament: an entirely abstract God, condensed within the centre of nothing other than an I-principle, stands at the centre of the religion of the Old Testament—an image-less I-God. How could this God first obtain a form that could be comprehended by a people living on the physical plane which they had to master?

Through a wise dispensation something remarkable originated in this regard in southern Europe. Emigrations had taken place from Asia and Africa; these mingled with other streams coming from the North. Those that came from the East brought the firm conviction of the worthlessness of maya, of the need to change the material kingdom of humankind into a kingdom of the spirit; and these mingled with others who had gained a stronger feeling of personality. And the strongest spiritual powers, that had remained behind longest in the emigration from West to East, met in Asia Minor and in the Greek and Italian peninsulas where the fourth cultural epoch developed, and the conquest of the physical world advanced by another stage. The mission of the third epoch, the Egypto-Chaldean, had been to perceive and comprehend the profundities of God. From it had to spring a people who were able to seek God in an abstract way, as a spiritual being with the least possible sensory content. Meanwhile in southern Europe another group was forming. Certain peoples had come down from the North, bringing with them their strong northern consciousness of personality. A union arose here between matter and the human soul. The result of this we see and admire in the art of Greece, in the temples of Greece, and in Greek tragedy, in which human beings began to depict their own destiny, secreting their own spirit in matter, incorporating it into outward realities. One might say that we have here a marriage between what is spiritual and what is physical, wherein each has an equal share. In all that the Greeks produced, spirit and matter had an equal share, and this was also the case in a certain sense with the Romans; they knew that spirit dwelt in them, that spirit could become personality in them.

It was only at this stage of human evolution that what had been foretold could assume actual form upon the physical plane. Christ could only descend to the physical plane once the human being had mastered it. A Christ would not have been possible in the old civilizations, when the physical plane was only seen as maya, and a longing for the past filled human souls. At the time the union occurred which we have seen represented in Greek art, the human being had turned more and more to the physical plane. This came to expression in the strong consciousness of the Roman citizen, and it was also the time when the Christ principle was able to appear in the flesh.

We have to consider all those who worked previously to the coming of Christ as being indeed acquainted with him, but we must look on them as Prophets who could only foretell; they beheld in the coming of Christ the fulfilment of what they themselves had striven for.

In the following lectures we shall see how Christianity is mingled with other elements in the era subsequent to the coming of Christ, and how this produced the conditions that now surround us. Today the period has been described when, through the conquest of the physical plane, human beings made themselves mature enough to understand the God made human—the Christ.

Lecture 10

STUTTGART, 14 AUGUST 1908

Changes in the Human Being's Relationship with the World of Spirit

In the last lecture we learnt that human beings had gradually conquered the physical plane during the post-Atlantean epoch. They had come gradually to understand that the physical world into which they had entered is the expression of the spiritual powers underlying it. We learnt also that when the Greeks and Romans were dominant in human evolution, human beings had established a kind of balance between their understanding of the physical and spiritual worlds. They had come to terms with the material world, learning gradually to understand and to love it. We must not think that such processes had no corresponding parallels in the spiritual world. Even if we go further back in human evolution we find that, as outward conditions alter in relation to human observation and perception of the physical world, conditions alter essentially also in relation to the other state of consciousness. So far we have described the nature of this consciousness primarily in relation to withdrawal from the physical body during sleep. We saw that in the Atlantean epoch human beings perceived only blurred outlines when awake, but that divine spiritual beings appeared before them when people exercised the dim kind of clairvoyance they possessed at the time.

But to understand the human being fully we must also consider the alternating conditions of consciousness connected with what we call death and what lies beyond death; we shall then see that the ordinary life we observe between birth and death has also an essentially different aspect. So far we have considered human destiny in the life between birth and death from the Atlantean epoch to the age of Greece and Rome; we must now inquire as precisely as possible into this destiny between death and rebirth, for the life of the human being continues after death. From the moment during the Lemurian epoch when we first entered into earthly incarnation, and life within a physical body first alternated with life outside it, the human being has in a sense led a twofold life, and possessed a twofold destiny—one upon earth and one in the spiritual world between death and rebirth. Though many think that change only happens in the physical world, and that everything between death and rebirth can quickly be characterized, this belief is absolutely incorrect.

Destinies change in the period of human development in the world of spirit also. We shall best understand how these changes occur if we consider the life the human being leads here in the physical world, and our relationship to the other kingdoms around us. At our present stage of evolution, we by no means exist in isolation but are related in diverse ways to all that surrounds us. Think only how our consciousness, our self-awareness, depends upon what surrounds us. If no other kingdom surrounded us, no mineral, vegetable, animal kingdom, if there was no atmosphere, no clouds which reflect the light to us, our I as it is now would not have been kindled by the outer world. Our capacity of conscious self-awareness is immersed during the day in the world that surrounds us. Between birth and death we are plunged into a certain environment through having an etheric and physical body. From the lower kingdoms of nature we derive the food giving us the substances and forces which pass through us. We can say that before birth and then also on entering earthly existence, we enter into connection with the lower kingdoms of nature. It is true that we only form this connection in so far as we assume a physical body, and then assimilate such substances as our means of support. In the physical world, therefore, the human being is not an intrinsic and self-contained being. Only think how we must continually inhale a certain quantity of air. We are by no means enclosed within our skin; our being extends into the air. On entering physical existence we enter into a certain relationship with the kingdoms below us; we dip down into them. On leaving the body we rise into higher kingdoms, those of the angels, archangels and archai, and indeed into still loftier kingdoms. Just as, through the needs of the physical body, we enter into relationship with the lower kingdoms, so after death we enter into relationship with higher kingdoms.

Let us now pass to the epoch when human beings first began to enter upon earthly incarnations. This was in the Lemurian epoch, when, though they did enter a physical body, they had very little connection with the physical world. They had as yet the merest trace of sense organs, and had therefore hardly any perception of the outer world. The human being actually passed through a condition at the beginning of his incarnations when his connection with the physical world was very slight; because of this he was all the more at home in worlds of the spirit. This was also the period when, having left the physical body—not only during sleep but also after death—the human being entered a world full of spiritual light where he perceived spiritual beings; where, to a certain extent, he drew strength from these beings as he now draws it from the physical world. It was a time when he reached out into the kingdoms above him as he now reaches out into the physical world. His being extended into the kingdom of the angels, archangels, and even into higher kingdoms which interpenetrate his own. Only at death did he gain an—albeit still dim—consciousness. He only drew into the physical world gradually, nourishing himself spiritually with the vision of divine spiritual beings. We only gained our I in the course of time as we passed through our various incarnations; we did not have it at an early stage. Other beings of whom we said that they had passed through their human stage at an earlier period already possessed an I, and the human being learnt to know the I through beholding them, but only came to know its full scope in the period between death and rebirth. When a person died at that time they had the feeling that only when they could see divine spiritual beings did they really begin to live. The further they sojourned in the period after death, the higher the stage to which they attained. They grew even more conscious until the time came (between death and rebirth) when the mighty being appeared who had first given true content to their life, and regarding whom they felt: 'From him I have come; I belong to him.' This was the same being, seen in a primeval period, who later incarnated on earth as the Christ. It was not possible in the Lemurian period for a human being to behold

Christ in a physical body, but he did behold him midway between death and rebirth; he thus became a part of Christ and knew him in the spiritual world.

As time passed on, humankind grew ever more conscious in the physical world. Full consciousness came first in the middle of the Atlantean epoch, but it came gradually. The more conscious human beings became in the physical world and the more the germ of the I had entered into them, the less did their consciousness reach up into higher worlds after death. At first they were no longer able to attain to the vision of Christ, but saw only angels and archangels, and later, in the Atlantean epoch, even this was denied them; it was only granted to those who were most advanced. In normal conditions human beings only perceived angels through their ancient dim clairvoyance: the deities which the Greeks recalled and addressed as Zeus, and the Germanic people as Wotan, were the same as the Christian angeloi.

We have already said that in the Atlantean epoch, during sleep but also especially in the time between death and rebirth, the human being was the companion of the gods. These gods were angels, or, at most, archangels, and only when someone had prepared themselves in this life by what they felt to be good deeds, was the vision of Christ vouchsafed to them under certain circumstances, mediated by these lesser beings. The human being still knew the Christ, however, through the deeds and the nature of the angels and archangels. Just as light is still light though tinted by passing through coloured glass, so the Christ-form was seen, but with waning strength. It was none other than the sun spirit who thus appeared with waning strength, waning because humankind was attracted more and more to the physical aspect of existence and had learnt to love it.

So humanity developed through the different ages of post-Atlantean civilization, and in each of them appeared the remembrance of earlier epochs which they had also actually once experienced. In the Egyptian age we find a memory of the Lemurian epoch. How did initiates at that time portray the life after death? They wanted people after death to experience—if only as a faint echo—what human beings experienced in olden times when they raised themselves up to a realm where they felt safely sustained: to that supreme being, the great sun spirit. This is the meaning of what the ancient Egyptians called the Judgment of the Dead,[21] when the dead person appeared before his judge, who weighed his deeds. If these were found to be worthy he might, through merit acquired in the physical world, become a part of the being revered as the god of light, the sun god. This was the being called Osiris. The journey to Osiris, the union with him, was what was intended to be imparted to the dead as a recollection of an actual previous evolutionary condition. This is how we must understand what is contained in the Book of the Dead, that most remarkable record of the Egyptian people.

In my book *Christianity as Mystical Fact*, due to prevailing conditions then, I could not yet describe the full esotericism of such things, which it is important to substantially deepen. According to the ancient Egyptian idea, if the deeds of a soul made it worthy of this vision, it might be united with Osiris; indeed it was actually addressed as 'an Osiris', through being united with him. The priestly words for this were as follows:

> Osiris was cleansed in the pool to the south of the field of Hotop and north of the field of locusts, where the gods of growth wash in the fourth hour of the night and in the eighth of the day, the image of the heart of the god passing from the night to the day.

It is impossible to express the full depth of meaning of these words but it is important to understand the expression, 'from the night to the day'. Previously it had been night; the soul is led over to a day—to a spiritual day—when it will be united with Osiris, when it may itself become an Osiris. The soul in this way actually experienced its destiny in another world, the world lying between death and birth.

Consciousness between death and rebirth increasingly dimmed, though it was never lost completely; it was never extinguished, though it grew faint. The more affection human beings developed for the sensory, physical world, the more they had to content themselves with the vision of lower beings, and the less it was possible for higher beings to commune with them. All the beings who were their good companions during the Atlantean epoch, when they were still clairvoyant, especially in the period between death and rebirth, faded away, and gradually the connections between the human being and those ancient gods was lost.

We know that remnants of ancient clairvoyance survived into later ages of European culture, that there were some people who in certain states of consciousness could still rise to vision of the gods. Such people also enjoyed a more vivid communion with the gods after death, had a more intimate life with them. Such a communion was good not only for these people themselves but also for the gods, for people bring with them the love they have succeeded in developing in the physical world. Thus the gods received back from them as sacrament and offering what they had acquired as love in the physical world. Yet human beings grew ever less fit for this communion with the gods, because their love for the physical world continually increased. The souls of those dwelling in the regions from which the Germanic peoples have since sprung, gradually possessed less and less vision of the gods, and therefore also had little fellowship with them between death and rebirth. This gave rise to the idea that the gods were losing their connection with the earth which they had themselves created, and losing also their dominion over it. This sense of things gave rise to the conception of the 'Twilight of the Gods'. This is what actually underlay it: the gods had to withdraw from the world they had themselves created. The gods who, even as late as the Atlantean epoch, had descended into the bodies of the most advanced human beings and had taught them important secrets in the mysteries, were obliged gradually to withdraw, and they could only engage with the physical world by using the more advanced human beings as their instruments or vehicles. This actually happened in the Atlantean epoch; and those who were initiated into the ancient Druid mysteries knew, for example, that a primordial Atlantean individuality known as Sig appeared for long after the Atlantean catastrophe in many diverse forms in European bodies.

All names such as Siegfried and Sigurd preserve exoterically a memory of the repeated appearances of this individuality who was finally only perceptible to those who had been initiated into the mysteries. He united himself with high initiates, and it became more and more necessary, the closer we come to our own epoch, for him to seek out those who had already passed through many incarnations in which they had purified themselves. Now, in order that we may understand our epoch, we must touch the hem of a great mystery which throws light on much that has taken place in our civilization. Let us turn once more to the middle of the Atlantean epoch, when the physical world was, we can say, first revealed to humankind. A sort of parting of the ways then took place for the gods—those who had been the ancient companions of human beings in higher realms. Coming from spiritual heights the human being had plunged ever deeper into the physical world. He had already passed through three great aeons, the third being the Lemurian, the fourth the Atlantean, and this will be followed by three others. We are living at present in the fifth aeon. The Lemurian age came to an end through great fire catastrophes, the Atlantean through mighty catastrophes of ice and water, while our age will come to an end through other forces, through a mighty increase of egotism in human nature, and, on account of this, through the war of all against all.

Only those who turn to a spiritual life will survive the catastrophe, the war of all against all, just as only a small group of people escaped from the catastrophes of Lemuria and Atlantis. The war of all against all will be still more terrible for those involved in it than were those of fire and water, however terrible we may picture them to have been. Those who are now turning towards a spiritual life should feel it their duty to do all that is possible to rescue the good seed of our age and carry it over into the sixth epoch, which will follow the present one. This fifth epoch is made up of great subdivisions: the ancient Indian, the Persian, the Egyptian, the Greco-Roman, and the present one, which will be followed by the sixth and the seventh, on into the time of the war of all against all.

We have at present passed the midpoint of Earth. Had human beings turned towards the spiritualizing of themselves before they had completely entered the physical world, the conquest of the physical plane, of which we spoke in the last lecture, would never have taken place. The human being has, however, taken a path leading deeper and deeper into physical evolution; he has gone beyond the point that would have represented the deepest stage if at that time he had turned back toward spiritualization. This point (in the middle of the Atlantean epoch) was an important parting of the ways for certain spiritual beings. They had then to decide whether they would sink into a kind of abyss from which they would rise again later all the stronger (for through their fall they would have developed greater powers) or whether they would take the direct way. Certain spiritual beings, those who had formerly been the companions of humankind, took the direct ascent; they decided never again to enter human bodies, but to remain in the realms of the spirit. The subsequent development of humanity passed them by with hardly a trace. There were, on the other hand, other divine beings, a number of whom have been preserved in the memory of the people of Europe and elsewhere under such names as Zeus, Wotan, etc.; they decided, for the salvation of humanity, to descend again and again into human bodies, so that they might work for humanity. It was not possible for all of them to descend to the same extent, for the human being had entered so deeply into the physical world that human bodies became ever less suitable instruments for divine beings. Only those human beings who had purified their bodies in a certain way—who, throughout the course of many incarnations had developed such noble etheric and physical bodies that they had completely banished from their souls certain connections with the physical world; who, through their whole disposition, had lived less in the earthly than the unearthly realm—only such people were still able to receive into themselves the souls of high spiritual beings as they would receive their own soul. So it happened that those into whom spiritual beings had entered could not, as it were, descend far enough into physical existence; they therefore held a very unique position in the world.

Let us picture such a being, one who for many incarnations had developed their bodily forces, had won an inner victory over it so that they lived more in the spiritual than in the physical world, and was, on this account, fitted to be the vehicle of a higher being. Was it possible for such a being to be fully understood by those who had descended completely into physical existence, who had developed a love for the physical world and sought to work on this physical plane? Would they not be better understood by those who had preserved the character of an earlier epoch, stragglers, as it were, from an earlier epoch? Yes, indeed, they could certainly be much better understood by ones who had survived from the Atlantean epoch. The Mongolian peoples have not descended so deeply, nor have they entangled themselves so much in the physical plane, nor done so much towards its conquest as the people of Europe. We see that external physical civilization is accomplished by Western nations rather than by the stragglers from Atlantean civilization who had remained in a sense stationary in their development, and were therefore not at home in a post-Atlantean world: they had instead retained certain earlier qualities, but had then degenerated.

It is often said that the Japanese are undergoing a significant development today through their own characteristic qualities. This is an illusion. They are not developing by virtue of their own qualities. In the last war against Russia they conquered with the help of battleships and cannon invented by Europeans; they made use of a foreign civilization. Progressive development only occurs when a people develops through its own intrinsic nature. It is on this that development depends.

Spiritual individualities who were still the companions of humankind in the Atlantean epoch could be understood better by nations who had in a certain way remained stationary, and who represented, in a later epoch, conditions beyond which the people of Europe had developed because of their individual self-awareness and feeling for freedom. Hence the teaching of these spiritual individualities had to be directed to such people, and we see here the consummation of a great mystery. We see beings who, when Europeans were at an earlier stage of evolution, were fully understood, incarnating and appearing later as teachers in the schools of initiation, and on this account being honoured as gods. We see Wotan, who had previously dwelt as an initiate in a human body and taught in the mysteries, being able, because he had not descended so deeply, to incarnate in a nation which, in a certain way, was backward, and on this account had preserved a feeling for the worthlessness of the physical plane, of its unworthiness as an expression of the deity, who looked on it as a place of sorrow and pain, and who held that the only real bliss was in leaving it. This individuality, known as Wotan, who had taught in the mysteries of the Teutonic peoples, is the one who appeared later as the Buddha, with the same mission. In the privacy of a group of students of spiritual science we can touch on such secrets. Buddha, who mediated between our world and the higher worlds, is the same individuality who once passed through regions of Europe and is remembered there under the name of Wotan.

We see from this how provision was made for those who had preserved certain tendencies and connections with earlier conditions. Knowing this, the historical fact of the good reception Buddhism received among the Mongolian peoples is comprehensible, and entirely in accordance with the wise guidance given to humankind.

Thus as humanity had to conquer the physical plane increasingly, it was no longer possible in a later age for such spiritual beings to incarnate directly in a physical body. It required a mightier spiritual being to do this, one who had been foretold by all earlier teachers. Even the ancient Egyptians when they spoke of Osiris recalled their connection with the ancient spirit of the sun, and said that the kingdom of Osiris would be established again upon earth.

For this to happen, a being of the nature of the Christ was needed. In withdrawing ever more from the kingdom of the dead (and we do really see him fading from life beyond the threshold), he had drawn ever nearer to this side of existence, until, in the fourth cultural epoch, he incarnated in a human body visible to all, but in a body that had been very specially prepared. The Christ principle could not assume a human body in the same way as those did who descended entirely to the physical plane. Even such a being as Jesus of Nazareth, who had passed through many incarnations and attained a high degree of initiation, was not capable at birth of being the vehicle of the Christ individuality. Only after preparing himself through a life of thirty years had he succeeded in so far cleansing and purifying the outward physical sheaths—the physical, etheric and astral bodies—that the Christ individuality could make use of them. In the thirtieth year of his life the individuality of Jesus of Nazareth relinquished the outer vessels which he had purified. This took place at the Jordan Baptism by John when, we can say, the individualities exchanged places, when the Christ took possession, not of an ordinary human body, but of a purified body.

Then followed three years during which Christ walked the earth in the body of Jesus, the years described in the Gospels between the Baptism and the Mystery of Golgotha. We have here an individuality who had not appeared as in the ordinary course of events, where a vessel is provided at birth that accords with the experience of many incarnations. Instead, because this individuality had entered into a body which for thirty years had been bound up with the physical world, and was now to receive a mighty impulse through the Christ, something of profound importance took place which esotericists can read in the Gospels when they really know how to read them. There it stands; but such things are veiled.

At the Baptism in Jordan, when the significant symbol of the dove appeared above the head of Jesus, who was not merely inspired but directly and immediately intuited by the Christ, something shot through the entire body of Jesus of Nazareth, even into those parts which, at the present stage of human evolution are most withdrawn from our human influence, the very bones. I am now saying something which to the materialistic consciousness of today seems nonsense; but that is of no matter. At the moment when the body of Jesus of Nazareth was permeated and fired by the individuality of Christ—the great sun spirit—the effect of this worked right into the bones.

If you burn a bone the cartilaginous part is consumed and the bone ash is left. The mineral substance of the bone and the cartilage are held together by a power which is opposed to fire, but also, therefore, associated with it. This power is at present entirely beyond the control of human will, but it was under the control of him who was later to pass through the event of Golgotha. Today we can move our hand, but we have no power to affect the chemical forces of our bones; we are anchored in and rooted by them. But the body of Jesus of Nazareth, through the Intuition of Christ, became the only one on earth that has ever acquired control over the force that holds together cartilage and bone-ash. Through this control over the bones a power entered the world which is truly able to conquer death, for human death must be ascribed to the bones. The human being has become entangled in the mineral aspect of the earth by being so fashioned that he has incorporated solid bony substance into himself. Death came to him because of this, and it is not without cause that death is represented by the very apt symbol of the skeleton. The Christ impulse is the living force that is able to again transform the bones: that is, to lead humankind gradually towards what is spiritual, which will come to pass in future evolution. This is why no external force was permitted to interfere with the skeletal structure of Jesus Christ: no bone of him was to be broken. The others who were crucified with him had their bones broken, but in him had to be fulfilled the words of the Prophet, 'No bone of him shall be broken!'[22] This was so that no external influence should destroy what had been given as a mighty, essential impulse for the earth.

In this way the mighty sun spirit worked at that time in the mystery which took place at the Baptism in Jordan. It was the same sun spirit who, through withdrawal from the earth, had made it possible for humankind to enter the ossification of physical matter. It now worked in such a way that we could receive the impulse which enables us once again to raise or spiritualize this tendency to ossification.

Risky as it may be to speak of such matters, it is the mission of the anthroposophic movement to declare those things that have always been known, taught, and beheld within the mysteries. Only because this mystery had been accomplished, and because of this alone, did another mystery become possible. We know that the several parts of the human body correspond to the levels or sheaths of the human being. The physical body corresponds to itself; the glandular system to the etheric body; the nervous system to the astral body; and the system of blood circulation to the I. The I entered in an externally physical way into human beings as they became ever more physically endowed with blood, thus becoming ever more capable of devoting themselves to, and engaging with, the material world. A time came when the surplus blood had to be sacrificed. Horrible as this may sound to the chemist, it is nevertheless true that the superabundant I, that would have brought humanity to the war of all against all through excessive egotism, flowed from the wounds of the Redeemer on Golgotha. At the moment when the wounds of the Redeemer bled, there was implanted within humanity the seed of the power by which it might raise itself again out of the state into which it had sunk so deeply.

If humankind had taken its upward turn again in the middle of the Atlantean epoch, it would never have attained full independence. Human beings had to conquer the physical plane, but then, on this plane, the impulse by which they could rise again had to be all the stronger—an impulse given by the Christ. Because the Christ was stronger he could not only lead mankind out of the depths, but could do something else, something of very great importance! A part of the world was conquered, mastered by humankind, a part that will be reunited with the spiritual world, led back to the spiritual world.

We saw in yesterday's lecture that during the Greco-Roman age humankind had progressed so far in the conquest of the physical world, had become so deeply entangled in it, that it needed a God in human form in order to recognize him. People could no longer penetrate to the spiritual world and perceive him there. Meanwhile conditions on the other side of life—between death and rebirth—had also changed. Because human beings had descended so much further into the physical plane, and developed so great a love for it, derived so much pleasure from it, what was on the other side of life became ever less perceptible to them. They retained a substantial memory of this world when they lived on the other side between death and rebirth, and much of this has been preserved in legend. When we read in Ancient Greek literature how the hero Achilles says: 'Better a beggar in the physical world than a king in the land of the shades,'[23] this fully expresses the feeling of that period. Because the human being had conquered so much of the physical plane, he longed to come back to it, for at that time he could not take much over with him. Only through Christ having come to earth, and through human beings having already experienced him in a preparatory way in the Old Testament era, only through receiving the Christ into their thoughts during life, could they take over with them what once again kindled light for them on the other side. What they took with them brightly illumined the other side of existence, and restored the Christ to them with even greater splendour than in this world. Hence we see how consciousness on the other side increasingly darkened as the time approached which we described yesterday, and how it then grew clearer again and more luminous as humankind came to know the Christ here. For what we learn of him in this world is not lost in the period between death and rebirth; we take our knowledge with us, and this is what the expression 'To die in Christ' means.

From what has been said you will see that throughout evolution the life not only of the living changes, but also that of the dead. Because the dead are nourished by what they have learnt here concerning the Christ, because they take the fruits of this with them to the life between death and rebirth, returning here again in ever-recurring incarnations, they will appear also in ever mightier, more Christ-filled bodies, and will make the earth increasingly into an expression of what Christ can be to a transformed world when in the future he leads the earth to higher and ever higher conditions. Thus we see how life, both on this side and on the other, combines to ripen the earth for what is to come; when the earth through being filled with the spirit of Christ will be united once again with the sun, and will thereby rise a stage higher in the cosmos. The Christ event—the coming of Christ—is therefore not only a fact of great importance to the human being, but is of infinite importance also to the evolution of the whole cosmos.

Lecture 11

STUTTGART, 16 AUGUST 1908

Relationships between the Cultural Epochs of Post-Atlantean Evolution

In the previous lectures we surveyed broad vistas both of human and also world evolution. We saw how mysterious connections in the evolution of the world are reflected in the developments apparent in civilizations in the post-Atlantean period, its cultural epochs. We saw how the first period of earthly evolution is reflected in the civilization of Ancient India; the second, during which the separation of the sun from the earth took place, is reflected in Persian civilization; and we have endeavoured, as far as time permitted, to sketch the various stages of the Lemurian period—the third in the course of the earth's evolution—in which human beings received the foundations of their I, which is reflected in the Egyptian cultural epoch. We saw that the initiation wisdom of Ancient Egypt was a kind of memory of this passage of humanity through earthly evolution. Then, coming to the fourth epoch, we find the true union between body and spirit beautifully depicted in the art of Greece, and saw this to be a reflection of what the human being experienced with the ancient gods, the beings we have described as angels. Nothing remained that could be reflected in our epoch—the fifth—the era now running its course. Mysterious connections do, however, exist between the different periods of post-Atlantean civilization; something we touched on in the first of these lectures.

You may recall it being said that the confinement of modern people to their own immediate, sensory surroundings, that is, to the materialistic belief that reality is only to be found between life and death, can be traced to the fact that the Egyptians bestowed so much care on the preservation of the bodies of the dead. They tried at that time to preserve the physical human form, and this has not been without an effect on souls after death. When the bodily form is thus preserved, the soul after death is still connected in a certain way with the form it bore during life. Thought-forms are called up in the soul which cling to the sensible form, and when a person incarnates again and again and the soul enters into new bodies, these thought-forms still endure. All that the human soul experiences when it looked down from spiritual heights upon its corpse becomes firmly rooted within it. The soul becomes fixated on this, unable to turn its gaze away from what is bound within flesh. The result has been that countless souls who were incarnated in Ancient Egypt are born again with the fruits of this vision, and can only believe in the reality of the physical body. This was firmly implanted in souls at that time. Things that take place in one cultural epoch are by no means unconnected with the ages that follow.

If we represent here with a line the seven succeeding cultural epochs of post-Atlantean civilization, the fourth epoch, which is exactly in the middle, occupies an exceptional position.

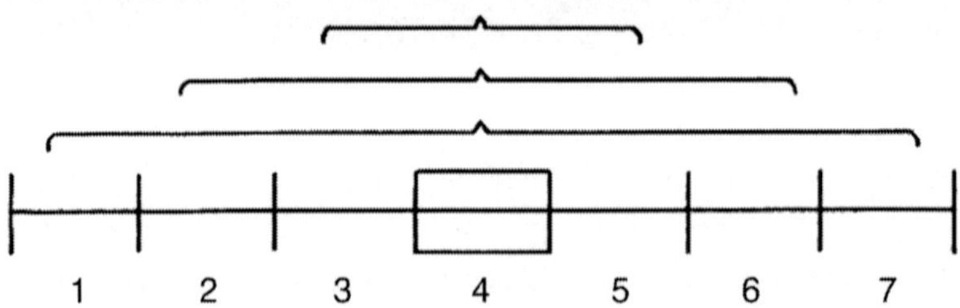

An exoteric survey of this epoch already shows us that it produced the most wonderful, external physical things which, we can say, show how humankind mastered the physical world in a unique and harmonious way. Looking back to the Egyptian Pyramids we observe a type of geometric form which demonstrates the symbolic meaning of certain things. The close union of spirit—the shaping human spirit—and the physical form had not yet been fully accomplished. We see this with special clarity in the Sphinx, the origin of which is to be traced to a memory of the Atlantean etheric human form. This physical Sphinx cannot give us any direct conviction of this union, although it is a great human conception; in it we see embodied the thought that the human being is still animal-like below and only attains to what is human in the etheric head.

What we encounter on the physical plane is ennobled in the fourth age in the forms of Greek sculpture; and the moral life, the destiny of man, we find depicted in the Greek tragedies. In them we see the inner life of the spirit played out upon the physical plane in a very wonderful way. We see the meaning of earthly evolution in so far as the gods are connected with it.

So long as the earth was a part of the sun, sublime sun spirits were united with the human race. By the end of the Atlantean epoch these exalted beings had gradually faded, along with the sun, from human consciousness. Human vision was no longer capable of reaching up after death to the high realms where perception of the sun spirits was possible. If we imagine the perspective of these beings, we can picture them saying: We were once united with humanity but had to withdraw from them for a time. The divine world had to disappear from human consciousness so as to reappear in a newer, higher form through the Christ impulse.

Someone who lived within Greek civilization was as yet incapable of understanding what was to come to earth through the Christ; but an initiate, one who, as we have seen, knew of the Christ in advance, could say this: The spiritual form preserved in human minds as Osiris had to disappear for a time from human sight; the divine horizon had to dim and darken, but within us dwells the sure knowledge that the divine glory will appear again on earth. Some possessed this cosmic consciousness of the withdrawal of divine glory and its return, reflected in Greek tragedy in which the human being, portrayed as an image of the gods, lives, strives, and has a tragic end. At the same time Greek tragedy holds within it the idea that the human being may still conquer through his spiritual power. The drama of the living and dying human being was at the same time intended to encompass humanity's whole relationship to the universe. In every realm of Greek culture we see this union between things of the spirit and things of the senses. It was a unique epoch in post-Atlantean civilization.

It is remarkable how certain phenomena of the third epoch are connected as by underground channels with our own, the fifth. Certain things which were sown as seed during the Egyptian age are reappearing in our own; others which were sown as seed during the Persian age will appear in the sixth; and things belonging to the first epoch will return in the seventh. Everything has a deep and lawful connection; the past always points to and contains within it seeds of the future. This connection will best be realized if we explain it by considering the two extremes, those things connecting the first and the seventh epochs. Let us turn back to the first cultural epoch and consider, not what history tells us, but what really existed in ancient pre-Vedic times.

Everything that appeared later had been first prepared in advance; this was especially the case with the division of mankind into castes. Europeans may feel strong objections to the caste system, but it was justified in the civilization of that time, and is profoundly connected with human karma. The souls coming over from Atlantis were really of very diverse qualities, and in some respects it was suitable for these souls, of whom some were at a more advanced stage than others, to be divided in accordance with the karma they had previously stored up for themselves. In that far-off age humanity was not left to itself as it is now, but was really led and guided in its development in a much higher way than is generally supposed. At that time highly advanced individuals, whom we call rishis, understood the value and qualities of souls, and the differences existing between their diverse kinds. Underlying the division into castes lies a well-founded cosmic law. Though this may seem harsh to a later era, in that far-off time, when humanity was spiritually guided, the caste principle was entirely suited to human nature. Those who arrived in the new age with a particular karma also found themselves in a particular caste, and equally, you could only rise above a particular caste by undergoing a process of initiation. Only by stripping off or shedding the cause of your karma, only when you lived in *yoga*, could you in certain circumstances overcome it and rise to a higher caste. Let us keep in mind the anthroposophic principle which states that we must leave aside all criticism of the realities of evolution and seek only to understand them. Whatever negative impression this division into castes makes on us today, there was every justification for it, and it has to be seen in connection with a far-reaching and just arrangement for the human race.

When someone speaks of races today they speak of something that is no longer quite accurate; even in theosophical works great errors are made in this respect. Theosophy teaches that our evolution runs its course in 'rounds', that each round is subdivided into 'globes', and each globe further into 'races', which develop one after the other—so that we have races in each epoch of the earth's evolution. But this is not the case. Even in relation to modern humanity there is no justification for speaking simply of the evolution of races. In the true sense of the word we can only speak of race development during the Atlantean epoch. People were so different in external physiognomy throughout its seven periods that one might speak rather of different genuses than races. While it is true that the races have arisen through this, it is incorrect to speak of races in the primordial Lemurian age; and in our own age the idea of race will gradually disappear along with all the differences that are a remnant from earlier times. We still speak of races, but all that remains of these today are relics of differences that existed in Atlantean times, and the idea of race has now lost its original meaning. What new idea is to arise in place of the present idea of race? In fact humanity will be differentiated in the future even more than in the past, divided into categories, but not through external imposition; through their own inner spiritual capacities human beings will come to know that they must work together for the good of the whole of society. There will be categories and classes however fiercely class-war may rage today. But among those who do not develop egoism but cultivate the spiritual life and evolve toward the good, a time will come when they freely incorporate themselves into humanity. It will be apparent to them that one person must do this, the other must do that. Division of labour will work right down into the smallest detail: work will be so organized that a holder of this or that position will not find it necessary to impose their authority on others. All authority will be freely acknowledged, so that, in the seventh epoch, in a small portion of humanity we shall again have divisions that recall the principle of castes, but are such that no one will feel forced into any caste. Each will say: I must undertake a part of the work of humanity, and leave another part to another—both will be equally recognized and valued. Humanity will be divided according to differences in intellect and morals; on this basis a spiritualized caste system will again appear. Guided, as it were, by mysterious channels, the seventh epoch will repeat what was prefigured in the first. The third, the Egyptian age, is connected in the same way with our own. Little as it may appear to a superficial view, all that was laid down during the Egyptian epoch reappears in the present one. Most people living on the earth today were incarnated formerly in Egyptian bodies and experienced an Egyptian environment; having lived through other intermediate incarnations, they are now again on earth, and, in accordance with the laws we have described, they unconsciously remember what they experienced in Egypt.

All this is reappearing now in a mysterious way, and if you are willing to recognize such mysterious laws whereby one civilization is connected to another, you must seek to uncover the truth rather than accepting all the legends and fantastic ideas presented as facts about human evolution. People think too superficially about the spiritual development of humanity. For example, it has been said of Copernicus[24] that someone with such ideas as his was possible because a change in thought about the solar system had arisen in the era in which he lived. Anyone holding such an opinion has never studied, even exoterically, how Copernicus arrived at his ideas about the relationships of the heavenly bodies. One who has done this, and who more especially has studied the great ideas of Kepler, knows differently, and will be strengthened even more in these ideas by what esoteric investigation has to say about it.

Let us consider this so that we may see the matter clearly, and try to enter into the soul of Copernicus. This soul had lived in the epoch of Ancient Egypt, and at that time occupied an important position in the rites of Osiris, knowing that Osiris was regarded as the high being of the sun. The sun was at the spiritual centre of Egyptian thought and feeling; I do not mean the outwardly visible sun, the latter being regarded only as the bodily expression of the spiritual sun. Just as the eye expresses and embodies the capacity of sight, so to the Egyptians the sun was the eye of Osiris, the embodiment of the spirit of the sun. The soul of Copernicus once experienced all this, and an unconscious memory of it impelled him to renew this ancient idea of Osiris, which at that time had been entirely spiritual, in a form possible for a materialistic age. When humanity had sunk more deeply into the physical plane, we meet this idea again in its materialistic form, as the Copernican theory. The Egyptians possessed the spiritual conception, and it was the world-karma of Copernicus to retain a memory of such thoughts, and this conjured forth the combination and compass of ideas that led to his theory of the solar system. Something similar was true of Kepler,[25] who, in his three laws, presented the movement of the planets round the sun in a much more comprehensive way; however abstract they may appear to us, they were the result of a most profound conception. A striking fact in connection with this brilliant mind is contained in a passage written by him, which fills us with awe when we read it. Kepler writes: 'I have thought deeply upon the solar system. It has revealed its secrets to me, and I will carry over into the modern era the sacred ceremonial vessels of the Egyptians.'[26]

Thoughts implanted in the souls of the ancient Egyptians meet us again, and our modern truths are the reborn myths of Egypt. If we wished to do so, we could trace this in many small details and particularities, following it back to the very beginnings of humanity. Let us think once more of the Sphinx, that wondrous, enigmatic form which later became the Sphinx of Oedipus, who uttered its well-known riddle. We have learnt already that the Sphinx is fashioned from the human form which, on the physical plane, still resembled that of animals, while its etheric aspect had already assumed human form. In the Egyptian epoch, human beings could only see the Sphinx in an etheric form after passing through certain stages of initiation. Then it appeared to them. But the important thing is that in true clairvoyant perception what you perceive does not appear before you merely like a lump of wood; certain feelings are necessarily associated with it. Under certain circumstances an unappreciative person may pass by a highly important work of art and remain unmoved by it; clairvoyant consciousness is not like this: when such capacities are truly developed the corresponding emotion is already aroused. The Greek legend of the Sphinx expresses an apt feeling, experienced by the clairvoyant during the ancient Egyptian period and also in the Greek mysteries, when someone had progressed to a stage where the Sphinx appeared to them. What was it that appeared before them? They beheld something incomplete, something that was in the process of evolving. The form they saw was in a certain way related to that of animals, and in the etheric head was perceived what was to work within the physical form in order to shape it to become more like the human form. What human beings were to become, what their task was in evolution, this was the question that rose vividly before clairvoyant perception of someone who saw the Sphinx—a question full of longing, of expectation, and of future development.

The Greeks said that all investigation and philosophy originated from longing; clairvoyants say something similar. A form appears to human beings which they can only perceive with their astral consciousness; it troubles them, it presents them with a riddle, the riddle of the future of humanity. This etheric form, which existed in the Atlantean era and lived on as a memory into the Egyptian age, is increasingly incorporated into the human being, reappearing in human nature on the other hand in all the religious doubts, in the impotence of our cultural epoch to address the question, 'What is the human being?' We have to see the Sphinx in all unanswered questions, in all statements that revolve round the '*Ignorabimus*', the inability to know. In ages that were still spiritual, human beings could rise to heights where the Sphinx actually stood before them, whereas today it dwells within people in countless unanswered questions.

It is therefore very difficult for people today to arrive at any certainty about the spiritual world. The Sphinx, which formerly existed outside them now dwells within them, for a being appeared precisely in the central epoch of post-Atlantean evolution who cast the Sphinx into the abyss—into the individual inner being of every person. Once the Greco-Roman age, with all its repercussions, had developed on into the thirteenth and fourteenth centuries, we arrive at the fifth post-Atlantean epoch during which, up to our own time, new doubts have arisen more and more in place of the old certainties. We encounter such things increasingly, and, if we wished, could discover many more instances of Egyptian ideas transformed into their materialistic counterpart in the new period of evolution. What has actually happened in the present age, we might ask, for this is no ordinary transmission of old ideas; we do not encounter these things as they once were, but in transmuted form. Everything appears in a more materialistic form. Even our human connection with animal nature reappears, but transformed into a materialistic conception. The fact that people knew in earlier times that they could not as yet fashion their body otherwise than in the semblance of animals, so that Egyptian memories gave rise to images of the gods in animal forms, is something we meet again today in the generally held materialistic view that the human being has descended from animals. Darwinism is nothing but an heirloom of Ancient Egypt in a materialistic form.

From this we see that the path of evolution has by no means been a straightforward one, but that something like a division has taken place, one branch becoming more materialistic and one more spiritual. What had formerly progressed in one line now splits into two lines of development, namely, science and belief. Going back into earlier times, to the Egyptian, Persian, and ancient Indian civilizations, one does not find a science separate from faith. What was known regarding the spiritual origin of the world passed in a direct line downward to knowledge of particular things. People were able to rise from knowledge of the material world to the most exalted heights; there was no contradiction between knowledge and faith. An ancient Indian sage or a Chaldean priest would not have understood this difference; even the Egyptians knew no difference between what was simply a matter of belief or a fact of knowledge. This difference became apparent once humankind had sunk more deeply into matter, had increasingly plumbed its material culture; yet for this to happen something else was necessary.

Let us suppose that this descent of the human being into matter had not taken place; what would have happened? We considered a like descent in the last lecture, but it was of a different nature; this is a new descent in another realm, through which something like an independent science arose alongside comprehension of spiritual things. This occurred first in Greece. Until then there was no opposition between science and religion, and this would have had no meaning to a Egyptian priest. Take, for instance, what Pythagoras learnt from the Egyptians, the lore of numbers. This was not merely abstract mathematics to him; it gave him the musical secrets of the world in the harmony of numbers. Mathematics, which is only something abstract to people of the present day, was for him a sacred wisdom with a religious foundation.

But humankind had to sink ever further into the material, physical plane, and it can be seen how the spiritual wisdom of Egypt reappears—though now transformed into a materialistic mythical view of the universe. In the future, the theories of today will be seen to have had only passing value, just as ancient theories have only a historical value to people today. Perhaps people will then be sensible enough not make the mistake of some of our contemporaries who say that until the nineteenth century humankind was ignorant of science, only then recognizing that all that was taught previously about anatomy was nonsense. In their view only modern discoveries are true. But in the future people may grow wiser, and will not see things in mere black-and-white. They will not reject our myths of anatomy, philosophy and Darwinism so disdainfully as people today reject ancient truths. Things which today are regarded as proven and firmly established are actually only transitory forms of truth. The Copernican system is but a transitory form, engendered through the plunge into materialism, and will be replaced by something different. The forms of truth continually change. In order that all connection with what is spiritual should not be lost, an even stronger spiritual impulse had to enter human evolution. This was described yesterday as the Christ impulse. For a time mankind had to be left to itself, as it were, as regards scientific progress, and the religious side had to develop separately; it had to be saved from the progressive onslaught of science.

Thus we see how science, which devoted itself to material things, was separated for a while from things spiritual, which now followed a distinct course so that the two currents—belief in what was spiritual, and the knowledge of external things—proceeded side by side. We even see in one particular period of development in the Middle Ages, a period immediately preceding our own, that science and belief consciously oppose each other, but still seek union. Consider the Scholastics who saw the tenets of faith as having been given directly and undeniably to mankind by Christ; and all the science which had arisen since science and religion divided they saw as serving only to prove this gift. Thus we see in the flowering of scholasticism an effort to employ all science to prove and affirm revealed truth. This school of thought held that human beings can gaze upwards to the tenets of faith and to a certain degree human science can imbue and penetrate them, but to do so, people must dedicate themselves to this endeavour.

But as time went on, all relationship between science and belief was lost, and there was no longer any hope that they could progress together, side by side. This divergence comes to a head in the philosophy of Kant, where science and belief are completely sundered. There, on the one hand, the categorical imperative is asserted, with its practical postulates of reason; on the other hand is purely theoretical reason which has lost all connection with spiritual truths and declares that from the standpoint of science these cannot be found.

However, another powerful impulse was already making itself felt, and this too embodied a memory of ancient Egyptian thought. Minds appeared that were seeking a union between science and belief, that were endeavouring, by entering profoundly into science, to recognize the things of God with such certainty and clarity that they would be accessible to scientific thought. Goethe is typical of such a thinker and of such a point of view. To him religion, art and science were one. He found religious experience palpably present in ancient Greek art and in turn, in his investigations of countless plant forms, rediscovered the great thoughts of the deity made outwardly manifest.

Taking the whole of modern culture, we have to see in it a memory of Egyptian culture; Egyptian thought is reflected in it from its beginning. The division in modern culture between science and belief[27] did not arise without long preparation. If we are to understand how this came about we must briefly examine how post-Atlantean culture was prepared during the Atlantean epoch. We have seen how a handful of people who dwelt in the neighbourhood of Ireland had progressed the furthest, acquiring those qualities which had to appear gradually in the succeeding epochs of civilization. As we know, the rudiments of the I had been developing since the Lemurian epoch, but that stage of selfhood in this small group of people, by whom the stream of culture was carried from West to East, consisted in a tendency to logical thought and the power of judgement. These had not existed previously; any thought that arose bore its own self-justification simply by virtue of arising. The beginning of a form of thought capable of discernment was implanted in these people, who bore the rudiments of this with them from West to East in their colonizing migrations, one of which went southwards towards India. Here the first foundations of self-developed thinking were laid. Later, this conscious thinking passed into the Persian civilization. In the third cultural epoch, that of Chaldea, it grew stronger; and with the Greeks it developed to a degree that enabled them to bequeath us the grand monument of Aristotelian philosophy.

Combinative thinking continued to develop, but always returned to a central point, where it received reinforcement. We must picture it as follows: when civilization entered Asia from the West, one group, which possessed only the smallest degree of purely logical thinking capacity, migrated toward India; the second group, which travelled towards Persia, possessed this capacity to a slightly greater degree; and the group that migrated towards Egypt possessed it still more. From this group there separated off the people of the Old Testament, who had precisely that combination of faculties that needed to develop to enable another forward step to be taken in this purely logical form of human cognition.

This is associated with the other thing we have been considering, namely the descent of humankind to the physical plane. The further we descend, the more does thought become merely logical, and the more it tends toward a merely external faculty of judgement. Pure logical thought, mere human logic, what proceeds from one idea to another, requires the human brain as its instrument; the cultivated brain makes logical thought possible. Hence external thinking, even when it has reached an astonishing height, can never of itself comprehend reincarnation, because it is in the first place only applicable to the things of the external sense world that surrounds us.

Logic may indeed be applied to all worlds, but can only be applied directly to the physical world; hence when it appears as human logic it is bound unconditionally to its instrument, the physical brain. Abstract thought could never have entered the world without a further descent into the world of the senses. This development of logical thought is bound up with the loss of ancient clairvoyant vision, and was bought at the price of this loss. The human task is to enhance and supplement logical thinking with clairvoyant vision. In time to come human beings will gain the faculty of Imagination as well, while still retaining logical thinking.

The human brain first had to be created, the human being had to emerge into the physical world. The human head first had to be fully elaborated in the likeness of the etheric head so that this brain could exist in us. Only then did it become possible for the human being to descend to the physical plane. But all spirituality could be saved only at a point of time *before* the last impulse to purely external, mechanistic thought had been given. If the Christ had appeared a few centuries later he would have come, as it were, too late, for humanity would have descended too far, would have been too much entangled in materialistic thought, and would not have been able to understand Christ. Christ had to come before this last impulse had arisen, when the current of spirituality and religion could still be saved as a current of faith and belief. Then the final impulse could be given, plunging human thought to the lowest point, where it was gripped and chained by physical life. This arose through the Arabs and Mohammedans. Moslem thought is only a distinct episode in Arabian culture and thought, which, in its passage to Europe gave the final impulse to logical thinking—to what is incapable of rising to the spiritual.

To begin with, the human being was so led by what we may call providence or spiritual guidance that spiritual life was saved in Christendom; later, from the South, Arabism approached Europe, which was to become the scenario for external culture—able to comprehend only what is external. Do we not see this in the arabesque itself, which remains a formal symbol incapable of rising to living form?

Humanity had first to be led down into matter, then in a roundabout way, via Arabism, the invasion of Arabic culture, we are shown how modern science first arose in what we can call the collision of Arabism with a Europeanism which had already absorbed Christianity. Ancient Egyptian memories had come to life again; but what made them materialistic? What made them into dead thought-forms? We can show this clearly. If progress had been straightforward, the memory of what had previously occurred would have simply resurfaced in our age. But now we see how the spiritual took refuge in faith while materialism gripped one wing of European culture. We see how memories of the ancient Egyptian age were so changed for us by their passage through Arabism that they reappeared in a materialistic form. Copernicus's modernity of outlook about the solar system was the outcome of his Egyptian memory. But the reason why he presented it in materialistic form, making of it a dead mechanical rotation, is because the Arabian mentality on the other hand drew this memory down into materialism.

From all that has been said you can see how mysterious threads connect the third and the fifth epochs. This can be seen even in the principle of initiation; and since modern life received a principle of initiation in Rosicrucianism, let us ask what this was. In modern science we have to see a union between Egyptian memories and Arabism, the latter focusing on what is dead. On the other hand, we see another union consummated between what Egyptian initiates imparted to their pupils and spiritual apprehensions. We see a marriage between wisdom and what had been rescued as the tenet and truths of faith. This wonderful harmony between the memory of Egyptian wisdom and the energy of the Christian impulse is found in Rosicrucian spiritual teaching. So the ancient seed laid down in the

Egyptian period reappears, not merely as a repetition, but differentiated and at a higher level.

Yet beside instructing us about the universe, earth and the human being, such thoughts must also enter into our feelings and our impulses of will, and give us wings; for they show us the path we have to travel. They point the path to what is spiritual, and also show how we may carry over into the future all the good that we have gained here on the purely material plane.

We have seen how paths separate and again unite; the time will come when, besides memories of Egypt uniting with spiritual tenets of faith to produce a Rosicrucian science which is at the same time a religion, separate from, and alongside a science that adheres to materialistic tenets, these two will also unite: science and Rosicrucianism.

When we turn back to the third cultural epoch we find this vividly prefigured in a Babylonian myth that tells of the god Maradu,[28] who meets with the evil principle of materialism, the serpent of the Old Testament, and splits his head in two so that in a sense the earlier adversary is divided into two parts. This was in fact what actually happened: a division of what existed in the ancient primordial waters, symbolized by the serpent. In the upper part we have to see the truths upheld by faith, in the lower the purely material acceptance of the world. These two must be united—science and what is spiritual—and they will be united in the future. This will come to pass when, through Rosicrucian wisdom, spirituality is intensified to become science, when it once more accords with scientific investigations. Then a great harmonious unity will again arise: the various currents of civilization will unite and flow together through the channel of humanity. In recent times it has been apparent, has it not, that such unity is being sought?

When we consider the ancient Egyptian mysteries we see that religion, science and art were then one. Cosmic evolution is figured there in the descent of the gods into matter, presented to us in grand, dramatic symbolism. Anyone who can appreciate this symbolism has science before them, for they find there vividly portrayed the slow descent of humankind into the world. We also encounter something else, namely art, for the picture presented to us is an artistic reflection of science. But besides these two, science and art, they become religion for us at the same time, for what is presented there pictorially is filled with religious feeling. These three were later divided; religion, science and art went separate ways, but now in our era already, people sense that they must again be reunited.

What else was the great endeavour of Richard Wagner than a spiritual striving, a mighty longing for an all-embracing cultural impulse? The Egyptians presented tangible pictures because the external eye had need of them. In our age this will be repeated: once more the separate streams of culture will unite, a whole will be fashioned, but now in a work of art whose primary elements will be the flow of musical tones. On every side we find connections, reflections between what arose in Egypt and modern times. As time goes on our souls will realize increasingly that each age is not merely a recapitulation but an ascent; that progressive development is happening in humanity. Then the deepest strivings of humanity—the striving for initiation—must progress and develop. The principle of initiation suited to the first epoch cannot be the principle of initiation for the altered humanity of today. It is of no value, if we are to ascend to the highest levels of initiation, to be told that the Egyptians had already found primeval wisdom and truth in ancient times, that these are contained in the old Oriental religions and philosophies, and that everything that has appeared since exists only to enable us to experience the same once again. No! Each age has need of its own distinctive energy and impulse within the depths of the human soul.

It is asserted in certain theosophical quarters that, while a Western initiation exists for our stage of civilization, it is merely a late product, and that true initiation comes only from the East.[29] We must reply that this cannot be decided without knowing something further. The matter must be studied more deeply than it is usually done. There may be some who say that in Buddha the highest summit was reached, that Christ brought nothing to add to Buddha; yet we recognize the key thing here only in positive, progressive evolution. If we ask those who stand on the ground of Western initiation whether they repudiate anything in Eastern initiation, whether their view of Buddha differs from that of the East, they answer, 'No'. They value it all; they agree with it all; but they understand progressive development. They can be distinguished from those who deny the Western principle of initiation by the fact that they know how to accept what Orientalism has to give, but in addition they know the advancing forms necessitated by changing times. They deny nothing that belongs to Eastern initiation.

Take a description of Buddha by one who accepts the standpoint of Western esotericism. This will not differ from that of a follower of Eastern esotericism; but a person with the Western perspective holds that in Christ there is something which goes beyond Buddha. The Eastern view does not allow this. If it is said that Buddha is greater than Christ that does not decide anything, for such matters require a positive outlook, a sense of evolution. In fact the Western standpoint is the same as the Eastern in regard to Buddha. The West does not deny what the East says, but it asserts something further. The life of Buddha is not rightly understood when we read that Buddha perished through the enjoyment of too much pork;[30] this must not be taken literally. From the standpoint of Christian esotericism it is right to say that people who accept such a statement at face value understand nothing about it at all: this is only an image, and shows the relation of Buddha to his contemporaries. He had imparted too many sacred brahmanical secrets to the outer world. His demise was due to imparting too many esoteric secrets to the world, as happens to all who impart such secrets. This is what is expressed in this strange metaphor.

Allow me to emphasize that we disagree in no way with Oriental conceptions, but people must understand the esotericism of such things. If it is said that this is of little importance, it is not the case. They might as well think it of little importance to be told that the writer of the Apocalypse composed it amid thunder and lightning; if anyone finds occasion to mock the Apocalypse because of this, we will reply: 'What a pity he does not know what it actually means when we hear that the Apocalypse was imparted to the earth "amid lightning and thunder".' We must keep in mind that Western esotericists never deny the Buddha, and that much that seemed puzzling as

Theosophy began has been explained by Western esotericism. The followers of Western esotericism never find themselves at odds with the mighty truths given to the world by H. P. Blavatsky. When we are told, for example, that we have to distinguish three aspects in the Buddha, the Dhyani Buddha, the Adi Buddha, and the human Buddha,[31] the Western esotericist can and does illumine such a statement. For we know that what is regarded as the Dhyani Buddha is nothing but the etheric body of the historic Buddha of which a deity took possession; that the being whom we call Wotan appropriated this etheric body. This knowledge was already present in Eastern esotericism, but was only first understood in the right way through Western esotericism.

The anthroposophic movement should seek to ensure that the feeling which rises in our souls from such thoughts as these should stimulate in us the desire for further development, that we should not stand still for a moment. The value of our movement does not consist in the ancient dogmas it contains (even if these be but fifteen years old), but in comprehending its true purpose, which is the tapping of fresh springs of spiritual knowledge. It will then become a living movement and will help to bring about that future which, if only very briefly, has been presented to your inward eye today by drawing upon what we are able to observe of the past. We are not concerned with the imparting of theoretical truths, but with strengthening our feelings and sensibilities into deeds. We have considered the evolution of universe, earth and human being. Let us try to encompass what we have gathered from these studies in a way that prepares us at any moment to embark on further development. What we call 'future', though, must always be rooted in the past. Will for the future must relate and correspond to knowledge of the past, but this past has no value if not changed into impulses for the future.

What we have heard has given us a picture of such mighty impulses that not only our will and our enthusiasm are stirred but our feelings of joy and sense of security in life have also been kindled. When we see how so many currents interweave, we have to say: Many are the seeds within time's womb, and all of them are to ripen. Through an ever deepening knowledge we must learn how better to cultivate all these seeds. We need knowledge, yes, but it should be in the service of active work, and in order to gain assurance in life. This must be the feeling that pervades all anthroposophic study. The 'theories' of spiritual science only reach their ultimate truth when they are transformed into life—into impulses of feeling and assurance in life so that we not only make theoretical observations but actually enter fully into the course of evolution.

Notes

For the cosmological explanations in this cycle, compare the writings *Cosmic Memory* (CW 11), and *Occult Science, An Outline* (CW 13). On the presentations about the Egyptian mysteries, see the lecture cycle *Egyptian Myths and Mysteries* (CW 106).

Textual basis: The cycle was recorded stenographically. However, the original shorthand is not preserved. The text was probably edited before going to press, but may nevertheless be considered reliable—even if not always word-for-word.

1 Congress of the Theosophical Society, 1907 in Munich. See further in *Rosicrucianism Renewed* (CW 284).

2 'Know Thyself': Inscription on the Temple of Apollo at Delphi.

3 'I am the I am': Moses: 2, 3, 14 (*Ejeh asher ejeh*).

4 After Plutarch, *On Isis and Osiris*. Inscription on the Temple of Isis at Sais in Egypt.

5 'You Greeks remain children all your life...': The story of the Egyptian priest who said this to Solon is related in Plato's *Timaeus*.

6 Arnold Böcklin, 1827-1901. The *Pietà* is in Basel.

7 Steiner uses the word somnambulem in German probably not to indicate physical movement so much as to point to a state—for which we have no word—to be contrasted with ordinary sleep.

8 Romans 8: 22.

9 Frederick Schiller, 1759-1805.

10 Francis of Assisi, 1182-1226.

11 Re. 'wonderful legend': see also *The Karma of Untruthfulness*, Vol. 1 (CW 173).

12 Torah, The Hebrew Bible: the five Books of Moses, the so-called Pentateuch.

13 Genesis 2: 7.

14 'Christ versus Luciferus': See also the lecture of 14 April 1912 in *Spiritual Beings in the Heavenly Bodies and in the Kingdoms of Nature* (CW 136).

15 Druid mysteries: See the lectures in Berlin, 1 & 6 May 1909, in *Wo und wie findet mann den Geist?* (GA 57), as well as Dornach, 10 & 14 September 1923, in *Initiation Science* (CW 228).

16 Matthew 10: 37-38.

17 Rudolf Steiner often quotes this statement from *Timaeus* (Chap. 8), but always reproduces it in the formulation of the Viennese philosopher Vincenz Knauer, with whom he was personally acquainted, from his work *Die Hauptprobleme der Philosophie in ihrer Entwickelung und teilweisen Lösung von Thales bis Robert Hamerling*, Vienna and Leipzig 1892, page 96 (belonging to Rudolf Steiner's library and underlined by him).

18 Pythagorus, 585-492 BC. The Pythagorean theory of numbers was based on the idea that 'the essence of things are numbers'.

19 Ernst F. Chladni, German physicist (1756-1827), who carried out fundamental research into the vibration of bodies.

20 Re. Siegfried: see also *Die Welträtsel und die Anthroposophie* (GA 54), *Good and Evil Spirits* (CW 102); and *Artistic Sensitivity as a Spiritual Approach to Knowing Life and the World* (GA 161).

21 'Egyptian Judgment of the dead': see *The Egyptian Book of the Dead.*

22 John 12: 36; refers to Moses 2: 12, 46.

23 'Rather be a beggar...': based on Homer's *Odyssey*, Book 11, where Odysseus visits the Underworld.

24 Nicholas Copernicus, 1473-1543.

25 Johannes Kepler, 1571-1630.

26 'Kepler wrote down the words': See his Preface to the 5th book of *Harmonices Mundi* (1619).

27 See also Rudolf Steiner's lecture (transformed into an essay) 'Human life from the point of view of spiritual science' in *Philosophie und Anthroposophie—Gesammelte Aufsätze*, 1904-1923 (GA 35).

28 See Rudolf Steiner, *Occult History* (CW 126).

29 'True initiation could only be obtained in the East': This refers to the already latent conflict between the Theosophical Society under Annie Besant, with headquarters in Adyar (India), and the German section of the Theosophical Society, under Rudolf Steiner. The following is from a letter by Édouard Schure: 'It was 1908... During a stay in Stuttgart I met about ten English, Dutch, French and Swiss theosophists. The following question was raised: "The two schools, that of Adyar and that of Dr Steiner, will they be able to come together?" We all thought that an understanding could be reached... A single person in the group protested. It was a Dutch theosophist ... an intimate friend of Leadbeater and Adyar. He expressly stated that the two schools would never be able to come to an understanding, and gave the reason that "India alone possessed the tradition and that there had never been scientific esotericism in the West".' (Quoted from: *Annie Besant und die Krisis in der Theosophischen Gesellschaft*, Leipzig 1913.)

30 That the Buddha perished from eating too much pork: Rudolf Steiner's remarks refer to a footnote in H.P. Blavatsky's *The Secret Doctrine*, 3rd Vol., p. 89, where it is said that the Orientalists did not understand the esoteric meaning of this legend of the death of Buddha.

31 'That in the case of Buddha we have to distinguish the Dhyani-Buddha': See H. P. Blavatsky, *The Secret Doctrine*, Vol. 3, p. 376ff.

Rudolf Steiner's Collected Works

The German Edition of Rudolf Steiner's Collected Works (the *Gesamtausgabe* [GA] published by Rudolf Steiner Verlag, Dornach, Switzerland) presently runs to 354 titles, organized either by type of work (written or spoken), chronology, audience (public or other), or subject (education, art, etc.). For ease of comparison, the Collected Works in English [CW] follows the German organization exactly. A complete listing of the CWs follows with literal translations of the German titles. Other than in the case of the books published in his lifetime, titles were rarely given by Rudolf Steiner himself, and were often provided by the editors of the German editions. The titles in English are not necessarily the same as the German; and, indeed, over the past 75 years have frequently been different, with the same book sometimes appearing under different titles.

For ease of identification and to avoid confusion, we suggest that readers looking for a title should do so by CW number. Because the work of creating the Collected Works of Rudolf Steiner is an ongoing process, with new titles being published every year, we have not indicated in this listing which books are presently available. To find out what titles in the Collected Works are currently in print, please check our website at www.rudolfsteinerpress.com (or www.steinerbooks.org for US readers).

Written Work

CW 1 Goethe: Natural-Scientific Writings, Introduction, with Footnotes and Explanations in the text by Rudolf Steiner
CW 2 Outlines of an Epistemology of the Goethean World View, with Special Consideration of Schiller
CW 3 Truth and Science
CW 4 The Philosophy of Freedom
CW 4a Documents to 'The Philosophy of Freedom'
CW 5 Friedrich Nietzsche, A Fighter against His Time

CW 6 Goethe's Worldview
CW 6a Now in CW 30
CW 7 Mysticism at the Dawn of Modern Spiritual Life and Its Relationship with Modern Worldviews
CW 8 Christianity as Mystical Fact and the Mysteries of Antiquity
CW 9 Theosophy: An Introduction into Supersensible World Knowledge and Human Purpose
CW 10 How Does One Attain Knowledge of Higher Worlds?
CW 11 From the Akasha-Chronicle
CW 12 Levels of Higher Knowledge
CW 13 Occult Science in Outline
CW 14 Four Mystery Dramas
CW 15 The Spiritual Guidance of the Individual and Humanity
CW 16 A Way to Human Self-Knowledge: Eight Meditations
CW 17 The Threshold of the Spiritual World. Aphoristic Comments
CW 18 The Riddles of Philosophy in Their History, Presented as an Outline
CW 19 Contained in CW 24
CW 20 The Riddles of the Human Being: Articulated and Unarticulated in the Thinking, Views and Opinions of a Series of German and Austrian Personalities
CW 21 The Riddles of the Soul
CW 22 Goethe's Spiritual Nature and its Revelation in 'Faust' and through the 'Fairy Tale of the Snake and the Lily'
CW 23 The Central Points of the Social Question in the Necessities of Life in the Present and the Future
CW 24 Essays Concerning the Threefold Division of the Social Organism and the Period 1915-1921
CW 25 Cosmology, Religion and Philosophy
CW 26 Anthroposophical Leading Thoughts
CW 27 Fundamentals for Expansion of the Art of Healing according to Spiritual-Scientific Insights
CW28 The Course of My Life
CW 29 Collected Essays on Dramaturgy, 1889-1900
CW 30 Methodical Foundations of Anthroposophy: Collected Essays on Philosophy, Natural Science, Aesthetics and Psychology, 1884-1901
CW 31 Collected Essays on Culture and Current Events, 1887-1901
CW 32 Collected Essays on Literature, 1884-1902
CW 33 Biographies and Biographical Sketches, 1894-1905
CW 34 Lucifer-Gnosis: Foundational Essays on Anthroposophy and Reports from the Periodicals 'Lucifer' and 'Lucifer-Gnosis,' 1903-1908
CW 35 Philosophy and Anthroposophy: Collected Essays, 1904-1923
CW 36 The Goetheanum-Idea in the Middle of the Cultural Crisis of the Present: Collected Essays from the Periodical 'Das Goetheanum,' 1921-1925

CW 37 Now in CWs 260a and 251
CW 38 Letters, Vol. 1: 1881-1890
CW 39 Letters, Vol. 2: 1890-1925
CW 40 Truth-Wrought Words
CW 40a Sayings, Poems and Mantras; Supplementary Volume
CW 42 Now in CWs 264-266
CW 43 Stage Adaptations
CW 44 On the Four Mystery Dramas. Sketches, Fragments and Paralipomena on the Four Mystery Dramas
CW 45 Anthroposophy: A Fragment from the Year 1910

Public Lectures

CW 51 On Philosophy, History and Literature
CW 52 Spiritual Teachings Concerning the Soul and Observation of the World
CW 53 The Origin and Goal of the Human Being
CW 54 The Riddles of the World and Anthroposophy
CW 55 Knowledge of the Supersensible in Our Times and Its Meaning for Life Today
CW 56 Knowledge of the Soul and of the Spirit
CW 57 Where and How Does One Find the Spirit?
CW 58 The Metamorphoses of the Soul Life. Paths of Soul Experiences: Part One
CW 59 The Metamorphoses of the Soul Life. Paths of Soul Experiences: Part Two
CW 60 The Answers of Spiritual Science to the Biggest Questions of Existence
CW 61 Human History in the Light of Spiritual Research
CW 62 Results of Spiritual Research
CW 63 Spiritual Science as a Treasure for Life
CW 64 Out of Destiny-Burdened Times
CW 65 Out of Central European Spiritual Life
CW 66 Spirit and Matter, Life and Death
CW 67 The Eternal in the Human Soul. Immortality and Freedom
CW 68 Public lectures in various cities, 1906-1918
CW 69 Public lectures in various cities, 1906-1918
CW 70 Public lectures in various cities, 1906-1918
CW 71 Public lectures in various cities, 1906-1918
CW 72 Freedom—Immortality—Social Life
CW 73 The Supplementing of the Modern Sciences through Anthroposophy
CW 73a Specialized Fields of Knowledge and Anthroposophy
CW 74 The Philosophy of Thomas Aquinas
CW 75 Public lectures in various cities, 1906-1918
CW 76 The Fructifying Effect of Anthroposophy on Specialized Fields
CW 77a The Task of Anthroposophy in Relation to Science and Life: The Darmstadt College Course
CW 77b Art and Anthroposophy. The Goetheanum-Impulse

CW 78 Anthroposophy, Its Roots of Knowledge and Fruits for Life
CW 79 The Reality of the Higher Worlds
CW 80 Public lectures in various cities, 1922
CW 81 Renewal-Impulses for Culture and Science—Berlin College Course
CW 82 So that the Human Being Can Become a Complete Human Being
CW 83 Western and Eastern World-Contrast. Paths to Understanding It through Anthroposophy
CW 84 What Did the Goetheanum Intend and What Should Anthroposophy Do?

Lectures to the Members of the Anthroposophical Society

CW 88 Concerning the Astral World and Devachan
CW 89 Consciousness—Life—Form. Fundamental Principles of a Spiritual-Scientific Cosmology
CW 90 Participant Notes from the Lectures during the Years 1903-1905
CW 91 Participant Notes from the Lectures during the Years 1903-1905
CW 92 The Occult Truths of Ancient Myths and Sagas
CW 93 The Temple Legend and the Golden Legend
CW 93a Fundamentals of Esotericism
CW 94 Cosmogony. Popular Occultism. The Gospel of John. The Theosophy in the Gospel of John
CW 95 At the Gates of Theosophy
CW 96 Origin-Impulses of Spiritual Science. Christian Esotericism in the Light of New Spirit-Knowledge
CW 97 The Christian Mystery
CW 98 Nature Beings and Spirit Beings—Their Effects in Our Visible World
CW 99 The Theosophy of the Rosicrucians
CW 100 Human Development and Christ-Knowledge
CW 101 Myths and Legends. Occult Signs and Symbols
CW 102 The Working into Human Beings by Spiritual Beings
CW 103 The Gospel of John
CW 104 The Apocalypse of John
CW 104a From the Picture-Script of the Apocalypse of John
CW 105 Universe, Earth, the Human Being: Their Being and Development, as well as Their Reflection in the Connection between Egyptian Mythology and Modern Culture
CW 106 Egyptian Myths and Mysteries in Relation to the Active Spiritual Forces of the Present
CW 107 Spiritual-Scientific Knowledge of the Human Being
CW 108 Answering the Questions of Life and the World through Anthroposophy
CW 109 The Principle of Spiritual Economy in Connection with the Question of Reincarnation. An Aspect of the Spiritual Guidance of Humanity
CW 110 The Spiritual Hierarchies and Their Reflection in the Physical World. Zodiac, Planets and Cosmos

CW 111 Contained in CW 109
CW 112 The Gospel of John in Relation to the Three Other Gospels, Especially the Gospel of Luke
CW 113 The Orient in the Light of the Occident. The Children of Lucifer and the Brothers of Christ
CW 114 The Gospel of Luke
CW 115 Anthroposophy—Psychosophy—Pneumatosophy
CW 116 The Christ-Impulse and the Development of I-Consciousness
CW 117 The Deeper Secrets of the Development of Humanity in Light of the Gospels
CW 118 The Event of the Christ-Appearance in the Etheric World
CW 119 Macrocosm and Microcosm. The Large World and the Small World. Soul-Questions, Life-Questions, Spirit-Questions
CW 120 The Revelation of Karma
CW 121 The Mission of Individual Folk-Souls in Connection with Germanic-Nordic Mythology
CW 122 The Secrets of the Biblical Creation-Story. The Six-Day Work in the First Book of Moses
CW 123 The Gospel of Matthew
CW 124 Excursus in the Area of the Gospel of Mark
CW 125 Paths and Goals of the Spiritual Human Being. Life Questions in the Light of Spiritual Science
CW 126 Occult History. Esoteric Observations of the Karmic Relationships of Personalities and Events of World History
CW 127 The Mission of the New Spiritual Revelation. The Christ-Event as the Middle-Point of Earth Evolution
CW 128 An Occult Physiology
CW 129 Wonders of the World, Trials of the Soul, and Revelations of the Spirit
CW 130 Esoteric Christianity and the Spiritual Guidance of Humanity
CW 131 From Jesus to Christ
CW 132 Evolution from the View Point of the Truth
CW 133 The Earthly and the Cosmic Human Being
CW 134 The World of the Senses and the World of the Spirit
CW 135 Reincarnation and Karma and their Meaning for the Culture of the Present
CW 136 The Spiritual Beings in Celestial Bodies and the Realms of Nature
CW 137 The Human Being in the Light of Occultism, Theosophy and Philosophy
CW 138 On Initiation. On Eternity and the Passing Moment. On the Light of the Spirit and the Darkness of Life
CW 139 The Gospel of Mark
CW 140 Occult Investigation into the Life between Death and New Birth. The Living Interaction between Life and Death
CW 141 Life between Death and New Birth in Relationship to Cosmic Facts

CW 142	The Bhagavad Gita and the Letters of Paul
CW 143	Experiences of the Supersensible. Three Paths of the Soul to Christ
CW 144	The Mysteries of the East and of Christianity
CW 145	What Significance Does Occult Development of the Human Being Have for the Sheaths—Physical Body, Etheric Body, Astral Body, and Self?
CW 146	The Occult Foundations of the Bhagavad Gita
CW 147	The Secrets of the Threshold
CW 148	Out of Research in the Akasha: The Fifth Gospel
CW 149	Christ and the Spiritual World. Concerning the Search for the Holy Grail
CW 150	The World of the Spirit and Its Extension into Physical Existence; The Influence of the Dead in the World of the Living
CW 151	Human Thought and Cosmic Thought
CW 152	Preliminary Stages to the Mystery of Golgotha
CW 153	The Inner Being of the Human Being and Life Between Death and New Birth
CW 154	How Does One Gain an Understanding of the Spiritual World? The Flowing in of Spiritual Impulses from out of the World of the Deceased
CW 155	Christ and the Human Soul. Concerning the Meaning of Life. Theosophical Morality. Anthroposophy and Christianity
CW 156	Occult Reading and Occult Hearing
CW 157	Human Destinies and the Destiny of Peoples
CW 157a	The Formation of Destiny and the Life after Death
CW 158	The Connection Between the Human Being and the Elemental World. Kalevala—Olaf Åsteson—The Russian People—The World as the Result of the Influences of Equilibrium
CW 159	The Mystery of Death. The Nature and Significance of Middle Europe and the European Folk Spirits
CW 160	In CW 159
CW 161	Paths of Spiritual Knowledge and the Renewal of the Artistic Worldview
CW 162	Questions of Art and Life in Light of Spiritual Science
CW 163	Coincidence, Necessity and Providence. Imaginative Knowledge and the Processes after Death
CW 164	The Value of Thinking for a Knowledge That Satisfies the Human Being. The Relationship of Spiritual Science to Natural Science
CW 165	The Spiritual Unification of Humanity through the Christ-Impulse
CW 166	Necessity and Freedom in the Events of the World and in Human Action
CW 167	The Present and the Past in the Human Spirit
CW 168	The Connection between the Living and the Dead
CW 169	World-being and Selfhood
CW 170	The Riddle of the Human Being. The Spiritual Background of Human History. Cosmic and Human History, Vol. 1

CW 171 Inner Development-Impulses of Humanity. Goethe and the Crisis of the 19th Century. Cosmic and Human History, Vol. 2
CW 172 The Karma of the Vocation of the Human Being in Connection with Goethe's Life. Cosmic and Human History, Vol. 3
CW 173 Contemporary-Historical Considerations: The Karma of Untruthfulness, Part One. Cosmic and Human History, Vol. 4
CW 174 Contemporary-Historical Considerations: The Karma of Untruthfulness, Part Two. Cosmic and Human History, Vol. 5
CW 174a Middle Europe between East and West. Cosmic and Human History, Vol. 6
CW 174b The Spiritual Background of the First World War. Cosmic and Human History, Vol. 7
CW 175 Building Stones for an Understanding of the Mystery of Golgotha. Cosmic and Human Metamorphoses
CW 176 Truths of Evolution of the Individual and Humanity. The Karma of Materialism
CW 177 The Spiritual Background of the Outer World. The Fall of the Spirits of Darkness. Spiritual Beings and Their Effects, Vol. 1
CW 178 Individual Spiritual Beings and their Influence in the Soul of the Human Being. Spiritual Beings and their Effects, Vol. 2
CW 179 Spiritual Beings and Their Effects. Historical Necessity and Freedom. The Influences on Destiny from out of the World of the Dead. Spiritual Beings and Their Effects, Vol. 3
CW 180 Mystery Truths and Christmas Impulses. Ancient Myths and their Meaning. Spiritual Beings and Their Effects, Vol. 4
CW 181 Earthly Death and Cosmic Life. Anthroposophical Gifts for Life. Necessities of Consciousness for the Present and the Future.
CW 182 Death as Transformation of Life
CW 183 The Science of the Development of the Human Being
CW 184 The Polarity of Duration and Development in Human Life. The Cosmic Pre-History of Humanity
CW 185 Historical Symptomology
CW 185a Historical-Developmental Foundations for Forming a Social Judgement
CW 186 The Fundamental Social Demands of Our Time—In Changed Situations
CW 187 How Can Humanity Find the Christ Again? The Threefold Shadow-Existence of our Time and the New Christ-Light
CW 188 Goetheanism, a Transformation-Impulse and Resurrection-Thought. Science of the Human Being and Science of Sociology
CW 189 The Social Question as a Question of Consciousness. The Spiritual Background of the Social Question, Vol. 1
CW 190 Impulses of the Past and the Future in Social Occurrences. The Spiritual Background of the Social Question, Vol. 2

CW 191	Social Understanding from Spiritual-Scientific Cognition. The Spiritual Background of the Social Question, Vol. 3
CW 192	Spiritual-Scientific Treatment of Social and Pedagogical Questions
CW 193	The Inner Aspect of the Social Riddle. Luciferic Past and Ahrimanic Future
CW 194	The Mission of Michael. The Revelation of the Actual Mysteries of the Human Being
CW 195	Cosmic New Year and the New Year Idea
CW 196	Spiritual and Social Transformations in the Development of Humanity
CW 197	Polarities in the Development of Humanity: West and East Materialism and Mysticism Knowledge and Belief
CW 198	Healing Factors for the Social Organism
CW 199	Spiritual Science as Knowledge of the Foundational Impulses of Social Formation
CW 200	The New Spirituality and the Christ-Experience of the 20th Century
CW 201	The Correspondences Between Microcosm and Macrocosm. The Human Being—A Hieroglyph of the Universe. The Human Being in Relationship with the Cosmos: 1
CW 202	The Bridge between the World-Spirituality and the Physical Aspect of the Human Being. The Search for the New Isis, the Divine Sophia. The Human Being in Relationship with the Cosmos: 2
CW 203	The Responsibility of Human Beings for the Development of the World through their Spiritual Connection with the Planet Earth and the World of the Stars. The Human Being in Relationship with the Cosmos: 3
CW 204	Perspectives of the Development of Humanity. The Materialistic Knowledge-Impulse and the Task of Anthroposophy. The Human Being in Relationship with the Cosmos: 4
CW 205	Human Development, World-Soul, and World-Spirit. Part One: The Human Being as a Being of Body and Soul in Relationship to the World. The Human Being in Relationship with the Cosmos: 5
CW 206	Human Development, World-Soul, and World-Spirit. Part Two: The Human Being as a Spiritual Being in the Process of Historical Development. The Human Being in Relationship with the Cosmos: 6
CW 207	Anthroposophy as Cosmosophy. Part One: Characteristic Features of the Human Being in the Earthly and the Cosmic Realms. The Human Being in Relationship with the Cosmos: 7
CW 208	Anthroposophy as Cosmosophy. Part Two: The Forming of the Human Being as the Result of Cosmic Influence. The Human Being in Relationship with the Cosmos: 8
CW 209	Nordic and Central European Spiritual Impulses. The Festival of the Appearance of Christ. The Human Being in Relationship with the Cosmos: 9

CW 210 Old and New Methods of Initiation. Drama and Poetry in the Change of Consciousness in the Modern Age
CW 211 The Sun Mystery and the Mystery of Death and Resurrection. Exoteric and Esoteric Christianity
CW 212 Human Soul Life and Spiritual Striving in Connection with World and Earth Development
CW 213 Human Questions and World Answers
CW 214 The Mystery of the Trinity: The Human Being in Relationship with the Spiritual World in the Course of Time
CW 215 Philosophy, Cosmology, and Religion in Anthroposophy
CW 216 The Fundamental Impulses of the World-Historical Development of Humanity
CW 217 Spiritually Active Forces in the Coexistence of the Older and Younger Generations. Pedagogical Course for Youth
CW 217a Youth's Cognitive Task
CW 218 Spiritual Connections in the Forming of the Human Organism
CW 219 The Relationship of the World of the Stars to the Human Being, and of the Human Being to the World of the Stars. The Spiritual Communion of Humanity
CW 220 Living Knowledge of Nature. Intellectual Fall and Spiritual Redemption
CW 221 Earth-Knowing and Heaven-Insight
CW 222 The Imparting of Impulses to World-Historical Events through Spiritual Powers
CW 223 The Cycle of the Year as Breathing Process of the Earth and the Four Great Festival-Seasons. Anthroposophy and the Human Heart (*Gemüt*)
CW 224 The Human Soul and its Connection with Divine-Spiritual Individualities. The Internalization of the Festivals of the Year
CW 225 Three Perspectives of Anthroposophy. Cultural Phenomena observed from a Spiritual-Scientific Perspective
CW 226 Human Being, Human Destiny, and World Development
CW 227 Initiation-Knowledge
CW 228 Science of Initiation and Knowledge of the Stars. The Human Being in the Past, the Present, and the Future from the Viewpoint of the Development of Consciousness
CW 229 The Experiencing of the Course of the Year in Four Cosmic Imaginations
CW 230 The Human Being as Harmony of the Creative, Building, and Formative World-Word
CW 231 The Supersensible Human Being, Understood Anthroposophically
CW 232 The Forming of the Mysteries
CW 233 World History Illuminated by Anthroposophy and as the Foundation for Knowledge of the Human Spirit

CW 233a Mystery Sites of the Middle Ages: Rosicrucianism and the Modern Initiation-Principle. The Festival of Easter as Part of the History of the Mysteries of Humanity
CW 234 Anthroposophy. A Summary after 21 Years
CW 235 Esoteric Observations of Karmic Relationships in 6 Volumes, Vol. 1
CW 236 Esoteric Observations of Karmic Relationships in 6 Volumes, Vol. 2
CW 237 Esoteric Observations of Karmic Relationships in 6 Volumes, Vol. 3: The Karmic Relationships of the Anthroposophical Movement
CW 238 Esoteric Observations of Karmic Relationships in 6 Volumes, Vol. 4: The Spiritual Life of the Present in Relationship to the Anthroposophical Movement
CW 239 Esoteric Observations of Karmic Relationships in 6 Volumes, Vol. 5
CW 240 Esoteric Observations of Karmic Relationships in 6 Volumes, Vol. 6
CW 243 The Consciousness of the Initiate
CW 245 Instructions for an Esoteric Schooling
CW 250 The Building-Up of the Anthroposophical Society. From the Beginning to the Outbreak of the First World War
CW 251 The History of the Goetheanum Building-Association
CW 252 Life in the Anthroposophical Society from the First World War to the Burning of the First Goetheanum
CW 253 The Problems of Living Together in the Anthroposophical Society. On the Dornach Crisis of 1915. With Highlights on Swedenborg's Clairvoyance, the Views of Freudian Psychoanalysts, and the Concept of Love in Relation to Mysticism
CW 254 The Occult Movement in the 19th Century and Its Relationship to World Culture. Significant Points from the Exoteric Cultural Life around the Middle of the 19th Century
CW 255 Rudolf Steiner during the First World War
CW 255a Anthroposophy and the Reformation of Society. On the History of the Threefold Movement
CW 255b Anthroposophy and Its Opponents, 1919–1921
CW 256 How Can the Anthroposophical Movement Be Financed?
CW 256a Futurum, Inc. / International Laboratories, Inc.
CW 256b The Coming Day, Inc.
CW 257 Anthroposophical Community-Building
CW 258 The History of and Conditions for the Anthroposophical Movement in Relationship to the Anthroposophical Society. A Stimulus to Self-Contemplation
CW 259 The Year of Destiny 1923 in the History of the Anthroposophical Society. From the Burning of the Goetheanum to the Christmas Conference
CW 260 The Christmas Conference for the Founding of the General Anthroposophical Society

CW 260a The Constitution of the General Anthroposophical Society and the School for Spiritual Science. The Rebuilding of the Goetheanum
CW 261 Our Dead. Addresses, Words of Remembrance, and Meditative Verses, 1906-1924
CW 262 Rudolf Steiner and Marie Steiner-von Sivers: Correspondence and Documents, 1901-1925
CW 263/1 Rudolf Steiner and Edith Maryon: Correspondence: Letters, Verses, Sketches, 1912-1924
CW 264 On the History and the Contents of the First Section of the Esoteric School from 1904 to 1914. Letters, Newsletters, Documents, Lectures
CW 265 On the History and from the Contents of the Ritual-Knowledge Section of the Esoteric School from 1904 to 1914. Documents, and Lectures from the Years 1906 to 1914, as well as on New Approaches to Ritual-Knowledge Work in the Years 1921–1924
CW 266/1 From the Contents of the Esoteric Lessons. Volume 1: 1904–1909. Notes from Memory of Participants. Meditation texts from the notes of Rudolf Steiner
CW 266/2 From the Contents of the Esoteric Lessons. Volume 2: 1910–1912. Notes from Memory of Participants
CW 266/3 From the Contents of the Esoteric Lessons. Volume 3: 1913, 1914 and 1920–1923. Notes from Memory of Participants. Meditation texts from the notes of Rudolf Steiner
CW 267 Soul-Exercises: Vol. 1: Exercises with Word and Image Meditations for the Methodological Development of Higher Powers of Knowledge, 1904–1924
CW 268 Soul-Exercises: Vol. 2: Mantric Verses, 1903–1925
CW 269 Ritual Texts for the Celebration of the Free Christian Religious Instruction. The Collected Verses for Teachers and Students of the Waldorf School
CW 270 Esoteric Instructions for the First Class of the School for Spiritual Science at the Goetheanum 1924, 4 Volumes
CW 271 Art and Knowledge of Art. Foundations of a New Aesthetic
CW 272 Spiritual-Scientific Commentary on Goethe's 'Faust' in Two Volumes. Vol. 1: Faust, the Striving Human Being
CW 273 Spiritual-Scientific Commentary on Goethe's 'Faust' in Two Volumes. Vol. 2: The Faust-Problem
CW 274 Addresses for the Christmas Plays from the Old Folk Traditions
CW 275 Art in the Light of Mystery-Wisdom
CW 276 The Artistic in Its Mission in the World. The Genius of Language. The World of Self-Revealing Radiant Appearances—Anthroposophy and Art. Anthroposophy and Poetry
CW 277 Eurythmy. The Revelation of the Speaking Soul
CW 277a The Origin and Development of Eurythmy

CW 278	Eurythmy as Visible Song
CW 279	Eurythmy as Visible Speech
CW 280	The Method and Nature of Speech Formation
CW 281	The Art of Recitation and Declamation
CW 282	Speech Formation and Dramatic Art
CW 283	The Nature of Things Musical and the Experience of Tone in the Human Being
CW 284/285	Images of Occult Seals and Pillars. The Munich Congress of Whitsun 1907 and Its Consequences
CW 286	Paths to a New Style of Architecture. 'And the Building Becomes Human'
CW 287	The Building at Dornach as a Symbol of Historical Becoming and an Artistic Transformation Impulse
CW 288	Style-Forms in the Living Organic
CW 289	The Building-Idea of the Goetheanum: Lectures with Slides from the Years 1920–1921
CW 290	The Building-Idea of the Goetheanum: Lectures with Slides from the Years 1920–1921
CW 291	The Nature of Colours
CW 291a	Knowledge of Colours. Supplementary Volume to 'The Nature of Colours'
CW 292	Art History as Image of Inner Spiritual Impulses
CW 293	General Knowledge of the Human Being as the Foundation of Pedagogy
CW 294	The Art of Education, Methodology and Didactics
CW 295	The Art of Education: Seminar Discussions and Lectures on Lesson Planning
CW 296	The Question of Education as a Social Question
CW 297	The Idea and Practice of the Waldorf School
CW 297a	Education for Life: Self-Education and the Practice of Pedagogy
CW 298	Rudolf Steiner in the Waldorf School
CW 299	Spiritual-Scientific Observations on Speech
CW 300a	Conferences with the Teachers of the Free Waldorf School in Stuttgart, 1919 to 1924, in 3 Volumes, Vol. 1
CW 300b	Conferences with the Teachers of the Free Waldorf School in Stuttgart, 1919 to 1924, in 3 Volumes, Vol. 2
CW 300c	Conferences with the Teachers of the Free Waldorf School in Stuttgart, 1919 to 1924, in 3 Volumes, Vol. 3
CW 301	The Renewal of Pedagogical-Didactical Art through Spiritual Science
CW 302	Knowledge of the Human Being and the Forming of Class Lessons
CW 302a	Education and Teaching from a Knowledge of the Human Being
CW 303	The Healthy Development of the Human Being
CW 304	Methods of Education and Teaching Based on Anthroposophy
CW 304a	Anthroposophical Knowledge of the Human Being and Pedagogy

CW 305 The Soul-Spiritual Foundational Forces of the Art of Education. Spiritual Values in Education and Social Life
CW 306 Pedagogical Praxis from the Viewpoint of a Spiritual-Scientific Knowledge of the Human Being. The Education of the Child and Young Human Beings
CW 307 The Spiritual Life of the Present and Education
CW 308 The Method of Teaching and the Life-Requirements for Teaching
CW 309 Anthroposophical Pedagogy and Its Prerequisites
CW 310 The Pedagogical Value of a Knowledge of the Human Being and the Cultural Value of Pedagogy
CW 311 The Art of Education from an Understanding of the Being of Humanity
CW 312 Spiritual Science and Medicine
CW 313 Spiritual-Scientific Viewpoints on Therapy
CW 314 Physiology and Therapy Based on Spiritual Science
CW 315 Curative Eurythmy
CW 316 Meditative Observations and Instructions for a Deepening of the Art of Healing
CW 317 The Curative Education Course
CW 318 The Working Together of Doctors and Pastors
CW 319 Anthroposophical Knowledge of the Human Being and Medicine
CW 320 Spiritual-Scientific Impulses for the Development of Physics 1: The First Natural-Scientific Course: Light, Colour, Tone, Mass, Electricity, Magnetism
CW 321 Spiritual-Scientific Impulses for the Development of Physics 2: The Second Natural-Scientific Course: Warmth at the Border of Positive and Negative Materiality
CW 322 The Borders of the Knowledge of Nature
CW 323 The Relationship of the various Natural-Scientific Fields to Astronomy
CW 324 Nature Observation, Mathematics, and Scientific Experimentation and Results from the Viewpoint of Anthroposophy
CW 324a The Fourth Dimension in Mathematics and Reality
CW 325 Natural Science and the World-Historical Development of Humanity since Ancient Times
CW 326 The Moment of the Coming Into Being of Natural Science in World History and Its Development Since Then
CW 327 Spiritual-Scientific Foundations for Success in Farming. The Agricultural Course
CW 328 The Social Question
CW 329 The Liberation of the Human Being as the Foundation for a New Social Form
CW 330 The Renewal of the Social Organism
CW 331 Work-Council and Socialization
CW 332 The Alliance for Threefolding and the Total Reform of Society. The Council on Culture and the Liberation of the Spiritual Life

CW 332a The Social Future
CW 333 Freedom of Thought and Social Forces
CW 334 From the Unified State to the Threefold Social Organism
CW 335 The Crisis of the Present and the Path to Healthy Thinking
CW 336 The Great Questions of the Times and Anthroposophical Spiritual Knowledge
CW 337a Social Ideas, Social Reality, Social Practice, Vol. 1: Question-and-Answer Evenings and Study Evenings of the Alliance for the Threefold Social Organism in Stuttgart, 1919-1920
CW 337b Social Ideas, Social Realities, Social Practice, Vol. 2: Discussion Evenings of the Swiss Alliance for the Threefold Social Organism
CW 338 How Does One Work on Behalf of the Impulse for the Threefold Social Organism?
CW 339 Anthroposophy, Threefold Social Organism, and the Art of Public Speaking
CW 340 The National-Economics Course. The Tasks of a New Science of Economics, Volume 1
CW 341 The National-Economics Seminar. The Tasks of a New Science of Economics, Volume 2
CW 342 Lectures and Courses on Christian Religious Work, Vol. 1: Anthroposophical Foundations for a Renewed Christian Religious Working
CW 343 Lectures and Courses on Christian Religious Work, Vol. 2: Spiritual Knowledge—Religious Feeling—Cultic Doing
CW 344 Lectures and Courses on Christian Religious Work, Vol. 3: Lectures at the Founding of the Christian Community
CW 345 Lectures and Courses on Christian Religious Work, Vol. 4: Concerning the Nature of the Working Word
CW 346 Lectures and Courses on Christian Religious Work, Vol. 5: The Apocalypse and the Work of the Priest
CW 347 The Knowledge of the Nature of the Human Being According to Body, Soul and Spirit. On Earlier Conditions of the Earth
CW 348 On Health and Illness. Foundations of a Spiritual-Scientific Doctrine of the Senses
CW 349 On the Life of the Human Being and of the Earth. On the Nature of Christianity
CW 350 Rhythms in the Cosmos and in the Human Being. How Does One Come To See the Spiritual World?
CW 351 The Human Being and the World. The Influence of the Spirit in Nature. On the Nature of Bees
CW 352 Nature and the Human Being Observed Spiritual-Scientifically
CW 353 The History of Humanity and the World-Views of the Folk Cultures
CW 354 The Creation of the World and the Human Being. Life on Earth and the Influence of the Stars

SIGNIFICANT EVENTS IN THE LIFE OF RUDOLF STEINER

1829: June 23: birth of Johann Steiner (1829–1910)—Rudolf Steiner's father—in Geras, Lower Austria.

1834: May 8: birth of Franciska Blie (1834–1918)—Rudolf Steiner's mother—in Horn, Lower Austria. 'My father and mother were both children of the glorious Lower Austrian forest district north of the Danube.'

1860: May 16: marriage of Johann Steiner and Franciska Blie.

1861: February 25: birth of *Rudolf Joseph Lorenz Steiner* in Kraljevec, Croatia, near the border with Hungary, where Johann Steiner works as a telegrapher for the South Austria Railroad. Rudolf Steiner is baptized two days later, February 27, the date usually given as his birthday.

1862: Summer: the family moves to Modling, Lower Austria.

1863: The family moves to Pottschach, Lower Austria, near the Styrian border, where Johann Steiner becomes station master. 'The view stretched to the mountains . . . majestic peaks in the distance and the sweet charm of nature in the immediate surroundings.'

1864: November 15: birth of Rudolf Steiner's sister, Leopoldine (d. November 1, 1927). She will become a seamstress and live with her parents for the rest of her life.

1866: July 28: birth of Rudolf Steiner's deaf-mute brother, Gustav (d. May 1, 1941).

1867: Rudolf Steiner enters the village school. Following a disagreement between his father and the schoolmaster, whose wife falsely accused the boy of causing a commotion, Rudolf Steiner is taken out of school and taught at home.

1868: A critical experience. Unknown to the family, an aunt dies in a distant town. Sitting in the station waiting room, Rudolf Steiner sees her 'form,' which speaks to him, asking for help. 'Beginning with this experience, a new soul life began in the boy, one in which not only the outer trees and mountains spoke to him, but also the worlds that lay behind them. From this moment on, the boy began to live with the spirits of nature . . .'

1869: The family moves to the peaceful, rural village of Neudorfl, near Wiener Neustadt in present-day Austria. Rudolf Steiner attends the village school. Because of the 'unorthodoxy' of his writing and spelling, he has to do 'extra lessons'.

1870: Through a book lent to him by his tutor, he discovers geometry: 'To grasp something purely in the spirit brought me inner happiness. I know that I first learned happiness through geometry.' The same tutor allows him to draw, while other students still struggle with their reading and writing. 'An artistic element' thus enters his education.

1871: Though his parents are not religious, Rudolf Steiner becomes a 'church child,' a favourite of the priest, who was 'an exceptional character.' 'Up to the age of ten or eleven, among those I came to know, he was far and away the most significant.' Among other things, he introduces Steiner to Copernican, heliocentric cosmology. As an altar boy, Rudolf Steiner serves at masses, funerals, and Corpus Christi processions. At year's end, after an incident in which he escapes a thrashing, his father forbids him to go to church.

1872: Rudolf Steiner transfers to grammar school in Wiener-Neustadt, a five-mile walk from home, which must be done in all weathers.

1873–75: Through his teachers and on his own, Rudolf Steiner has many wonderful experiences with science and mathematics. Outside school, he teaches himself analytic geometry, trigonometry, differential equations, and calculus.

1876: Rudolf Steiner begins tutoring other students. He learns bookbinding from his father. He also teaches himself stenography.

1877: Rudolf Steiner discovers Kant's *Critique of Pure Reason,* which he reads and rereads. He also discovers and reads von Rotteck's *World History.*

1878: He studies extensively in contemporary psychology and philosophy.

1879: Rudolf Steiner graduates from high school with honours. His father is transferred to Inzersdorf, near Vienna. He uses his first visit to Vienna 'to purchase a great number of philosophy books'—Kant, Fichte, Schelling, and Hegel, as well as numerous histories of philosophy. His aim: to find a path from the 'I' to nature.

October 1879–1883: Rudolf Steiner attends the Technical College in Vienna—to study mathematics, chemistry, physics, mineralogy, botany, zoology, biology, geology, and mechanics—with a scholarship. He also attends lectures in history and literature, while avidly reading philosophy on his own. His two favourite professors are Karl Julius Schröer (German language and literature) and Edmund Reitlinger (physics). He also audits lectures by Robert Zimmermann on aesthetics and Franz Brentano on philosophy. During this year he begins his friendship with Moritz Zitter (1861–1921), who will help support him financially when he is in Berlin.

1880: Rudolf Steiner attends lectures on Schiller and Goethe by Karl Julius Schröer, who becomes his mentor. Also 'through a remarkable combination of circumstances,' he meets Felix Koguzki, a 'herb gatherer' and healer, who could 'see deeply into the secrets of nature'. Rudolf Steiner will meet and study with this 'emissary of the Master' throughout his time in Vienna.

1881: January: '... I didn't sleep a wink. I was busy with philosophical problems until about 12:30 a.m. Then, finally, I threw myself down on my couch. All my striving during the previous year had been to research whether the following statement by Schelling was true or not: *Within everyone dwells a secret, marvellous capacity to draw back from the stream of time—out of the self clothed in all that comes to us from outside—into our innermost being and there, in the immutable form of the Eternal, to look into ourselves.* I believe, and I am still quite certain of it, that I discovered this capacity in myself; I had long had an inkling of it. Now the whole of idealist philosophy stood before me in modified form. What's a sleepless night compared to that!'

Rudolf Steiner begins communicating with leading thinkers of the day, who send him books in return, which he reads eagerly.

July: 'I am not one of those who dives into the day like an animal in human form. I pursue a quite specific goal, an idealistic aim—knowledge of the truth! This cannot be done offhandedly. It requires the greatest striving in the world, free of all egotism, and equally of all resignation.'

August: Steiner puts down on paper for the first time thoughts for a 'Philosophy of Freedom.' 'The striving for the absolute: this human yearning is freedom.' He also seeks to outline a 'peasant philosophy,' describing what the worldview of a 'peasant'—one who lives close to the earth and the old ways—really is.

1881–1882: Felix Koguzki, the herb gatherer, reveals himself to be the envoy of another, higher initiatory personality, who instructs Rudolf Steiner to penetrate Fichte's philosophy and to master modern scientific thinking as a preparation for right entry into the spirit. This 'Master' also teaches him the double (evolutionary and involutionary) nature of time.

1882: Through the offices of Karl Julius Schröer, Rudolf Steiner is asked by Joseph Kürschner to edit Goethe's scientific works for the *Deutschen National-Literatur* edition. He writes 'A Possible Critique of Atomistic Concepts' and sends it to Friedrich Theodor Vischer.

1883: Rudolf Steiner completes his college studies and begins work on the Goethe project.

1884: First volume of Goethe's *Scientific Writings* (CW 1) appears (March). He lectures on Goethe and Lessing, and Goethe's approach to science. In July, he enters the household of Ladislaus and Pauline Specht as tutor to the four Specht boys. He will live there until 1890. At this time, he meets Josef Breuer (1842–1925), the co-author with Sigmund Freud of *Studies in Hysteria,* who is the Specht family doctor.

1885: While continuing to edit Goethe's writings, Rudolf Steiner reads deeply in contemporary philosophy (Eduard von Hartmann, Johannes Volkelt, and Richard Wahle, among others).

1886: May: Rudolf Steiner sends Kürschner the manuscript of *Outlines of Goethe's Theory of Knowledge* (CW 2), which appears in October, and which he sends out widely. He also meets the poet Marie Eugenie Delle Grazie and writes 'Nature and Our Ideals' for her. He attends her salon, where he meets many priests, theologians, and philosophers, who will become his friends. Meanwhile, the director of the Goethe Archive in Weimar requests his collaboration with the *Sophien* edition of Goethe's works, particularly the writings on colour.

1887: At the beginning of the year, Rudolf Steiner is very sick. As the year progresses and his health improves, he becomes increasingly 'a man of letters,' lecturing, writing essays, and taking part in Austrian cultural life. In August–September, the second volume of Goethe's *Scientific Writings* appears.

1888: January–July: Rudolf Steiner assumes editorship of the 'German Weekly' *(Deutsche Wochenschrift)*. He begins lecturing more intensively, giving, for example, a lecture titled 'Goethe as Father of a New Aesthetics.' He meets and becomes soul friends with Friedrich Eckstein (1861–1939), a vegetarian, philosopher of symbolism, alchemist, and musician, who will introduce him to various spiritual currents (including Theosophy) and with whom he will meditate and interpret esoteric and alchemical texts.

1889: Rudolf Steiner first reads Nietzsche *(Beyond Good and Evil)*. He encounters Theosophy again and learns of Madame Blavatsky in the theosophical circle around Marie Lang (1858–1934). Here he also meets well-known figures of Austrian life, as well as esoteric figures like the occultist Franz Hartmann and Karl Leinigen-Billigen (translator of C.G. Harrison's *The Transcendental Universe*). During this period, Steiner first reads A.P. Sinnett's *Esoteric Buddhism* and Mabel Collins's *Light on the Path*. He also begins travelling, visiting Budapest, Weimar, and Berlin (where he meets philosopher Eduard von Hartmann).

1890: Rudolf Steiner finishes Volume 3 of Goethe's scientific writings. He begins his doctoral dissertation, which will become *Truth and Science* (CW 3). He also meets the poet and feminist Rosa Mayreder (1858–1938), with whom he can exchange his most intimate thoughts. In September, Rudolf Steiner moves to Weimar to work in the Goethe-Schiller Archive.

1891: Volume 3 of the Kürschner edition of Goethe appears. Meanwhile, Rudolf Steiner edits Goethe's studies in mineralogy and scientific writings for the *Sophien* edition. He meets Ludwig Laistner of the Cotta Publishing Company, who asks for a book on the basic question of metaphysics. From this will result, ultimately, *The Philosophy of Freedom* (CW 4), which will be published not by Cotta but by Emil Felber. In October, Rudolf Steiner takes the oral exam for a doctorate in philosophy, mathematics, and mechanics at Rostock University, receiving his doctorate on the twenty-sixth. In November, he gives his first lecture on Goethe's 'Fairy Tale' in Vienna.

1892: Rudolf Steiner continues work at the Goethe-Schiller Archive and on his *Philosophy of Freedom*. *Truth and Science*, his doctoral dissertation, is published. Steiner undertakes to write Introductions to books on Schopenhauer and Jean Paul for Cotta. At year's end, he finds lodging with Anna Eunike, née Schulz (1853–1911), a widow with four daughters and a son. He also develops a friendship with Otto Erich Hartleben (1864–1905) with whom he shares literary interests.

1893: Rudolf Steiner begins his habit of producing many reviews and articles. In March, he gives a lecture titled 'Hypnotism, with Reference to Spiritism.' In September, volume 4 of the Kürschner edition is completed. In November, *The Philosophy of Freedom* appears. This year, too, he meets John Henry Mackay (1864–1933), the anarchist, and Max Stirner, a scholar and biographer.

1894: Rudolf Steiner meets Elisabeth Fürster Nietzsche, the philosopher's sister, and begins to read Nietzsche in earnest, beginning with the as yet unpublished *Antichrist*. He also meets Ernst Haeckel (1834–1919). In the fall, he begins to write *Nietzsche, A Fighter against His Time* (CW 5).

1895: May, *Nietzsche, A Fighter against His Time* appears.

1896: January 22: Rudolf Steiner sees Friedrich Nietzsche for the first and only time. Moves between the Nietzsche and the Goethe-Schiller

Archives, where he completes his work before year's end. He falls out with Elisabeth Förster Nietzsche, thus ending his association with the Nietzsche Archive.

1897: Rudolf Steiner finishes the manuscript of *Goethe's Worldview* (CW 6). He moves to Berlin with Anna Eunike and begins editorship of the *Magazin für Literatur.* From now on, Steiner will write countless reviews, literary and philosophical articles, and so on. He begins lecturing at the 'Free Literary Society.' In September, he attends the Zionist Congress in Basel. He sides with Dreyfus in the Dreyfus affair.

1898: Rudolf Steiner is very active as an editor in the political, artistic, and theatrical life of Berlin. He becomes friendly with John Henry Mackay and poet Ludwig Jacobowski (1868–1900). He joins Jacobowski's circle of writers, artists, and scientists—'The Coming Ones' (*Die Kommenden*)—and contributes lectures to the group until 1903. He also lectures at the 'League for College Pedagogy.' He writes an article for Goethe's sesquicentennial, 'Goethe's Secret Revelation,' on the 'Fairy Tale of the Green Snake and the Beautiful Lily.'

1898–99: 'This was a trying time for my soul as I looked at Christianity. . . . I was able to progress only by contemplating, by means of spiritual perception, the evolution of Christianity. . . . Conscious knowledge of real Christianity began to dawn in me around the turn of the century. This seed continued to develop. My soul trial occurred shortly before the beginning of the twentieth century. It was decisive for my soul's development that I stood spiritually before the Mystery of Golgotha in a deep and solemn celebration of knowledge.'

1899: Rudolf Steiner begins teaching and giving lectures and lecture cycles at the Workers' College, founded by Wilhelm Liebknecht (1826–1900). He will continue to do so until 1904. Writes: *Literature and Spiritual Life in the Nineteenth Century; Individualism in Philosophy; Haeckel and His Opponents; Poetry in the Present;* and begins what will become (fifteen years later) *The Riddles of Philosophy* (CW 18). He also meets many artists and writers, including Käthe Kollwitz, Stefan Zweig, and Rainer Maria Rilke. On October 31, he marries Anna Eunike.

1900: 'I thought that the turn of the century must bring humanity a new light. It seemed to me that the separation of human thinking and willing from the spirit had peaked. A turn or reversal of direction in human evolution seemed to me a necessity.' Rudolf Steiner finishes *World and Life Views in the Nineteenth Century* (the second part of what will become *The Riddles of Philosophy*) and dedicates it to

Ernst Haeckel. It is published in March. He continues lecturing at *Die Kommenden,* whose leadership he assumes after the death of Jacobowski. Also, he gives the Gutenberg Jubilee lecture before 7,000 typesetters and printers. In September, Rudolf Steiner is invited by Count and Countess Brockdorff to lecture in the Theosophical Library. His first lecture is on Nietzsche. His second lecture is titled 'Goethe's Secret Revelation.' October 6, he begins a lecture cycle on the mystics that will become *Mystics after Modernism* (CW 7). November–December: 'Marie von Sivers appears in the audience. . . .' Also in November, Steiner gives his first lecture at the Giordano Bruno Bund (where he will continue to lecture until May, 1905). He speaks on Bruno and modern Rome, focusing on the importance of the philosophy of Thomas Aquinas as monism.

1901: In continual financial straits, Rudolf Steiner's early friends Moritz Zitter and Rosa Mayreder help support him. In October, he begins the lecture cycle *Christianity as Mystical Fact* (CW 8) at the Theosophical Library. In November, he gives his first 'theosophical lecture' on Goethe's 'Fairy Tale' in Hamburg at the invitation of Wilhelm Hubbe-Schleiden. He also attends a gathering to celebrate the founding of the Theosophical Society at Count and Countess Brockdorff's. He gives a lecture cycle, 'From Buddha to Christ,' for the circle of the *Kommenden.* November 17, Marie von Sivers asks Rudolf Steiner if Theosophy needs a Western–Christian spiritual movement (to complement Theosophy's Eastern emphasis). 'The question was posed. Now, following spiritual laws, I could begin to give an answer. . . .' In December, Rudolf Steiner writes his first article for a theosophical publication. At year's end, the Brockdorffs and possibly Wilhelm Hubbe-Schleiden ask Rudolf Steiner to join the Theosophical Society and undertake the leadership of the German section. Rudolf Steiner agrees, on the condition that Marie von Sivers (then in Italy) work with him.

1902: Beginning in January, Rudolf Steiner attends the opening of the Workers' School in Spandau with Rosa Luxemberg (1870–1919). January 17, Rudolf Steiner joins the Theosophical Society. In April, he is asked to become general secretary of the German Section of the theosophical Society, and works on preparations for its founding. In July, he visits London for a theosophical congress. He meets Bertram Keightly, G.R.S. Mead, A.P. Sinnett, and Annie Besant, among others. In September, *Christianity as Mystical Fact* appears. In October, Rudolf Steiner gives his first public lecture on Theosophy ('Monism and Theosophy') to about three hundred people at the Giordano Bruno Bund. On October 19–21, the

German Section of the Theosophical Society has its first meeting; Rudolf Steiner is the general secretary, and Annie Besant attends. Steiner lectures on practical karma studies. On October 23, Annie Besant inducts Rudolf Steiner into the Esoteric School of the Theosophical Society. On October 25, Steiner begins a weekly series of lectures: 'The Field of Theosophy.' During this year, Rudolf Steiner also first meets Ita Wegman (1876–1943), who will become his close collaborator in his final years.

1903: Rudolf Steiner holds about 300 lectures and seminars. In May, the first issue of the periodical *Luzifer* appears. In June, Rudolf Steiner visits London for the first meeting of the Federation of the European Sections of the Theosophical Society, where he meets Colonel Olcott. He begins to write *Theosophy* (CW 9).

1904: Rudolf Steiner continues lecturing at the Workers' College and elsewhere (about 90 lectures), while lecturing intensively all over Germany among theosophists (about 140 lectures). In February, he meets Carl Unger (1878–1929), who will become a member of the board of the Anthroposophical Society (1913). In March, he meets Michael Bauer (1871–1929), a Christian mystic, who will also be on the board. In May, *Theosophy* appears, with the dedication: 'To the spirit of Giordano Bruno.' Rudolf Steiner and Marie von Sivers visit London for meetings with Annie Besant. June: Rudolf Steiner and Marie von Sivers attend the meeting of the Federation of European Sections of the Theosophical Society in Amsterdam. In July, Steiner begins the articles in *Luzifer-Gnosis* that will become *How to Know Higher Worlds* (CW 10) and *Cosmic Memory* (CW 11). In September, Annie Besant visits Germany. In December, Steiner lectures on Freemasonry. He mentions the High Grade Masonry derived from John Yarker and represented by Theodore Reuss and Karl Kellner as a blank slate 'into which a good image could be placed'.

1905: This year, Steiner ends his non-theosophical lecturing activity. Supported by Marie von Sivers, his theosophical lecturing—both in public and in the Theosophical Society—increases significantly: 'The German Theosophical Movement is of exceptional importance.' Steiner recommends reading, among others, Fichte, Jacob Boehme, and Angelus Silesius. He begins to introduce Christian themes into Theosophy. He also begins to work with doctors (Felix Peipers and Ludwig Noll). In July, he is in London for the Federation of European Sections, where he attends a lecture by Annie Besant: 'I have seldom seen Mrs Besant speak in so inward and heartfelt a manner... Through Mrs Besant I have found the way to H.P. Blavatsky.' September to October, he gives a course of 31 lectures for a small group of esoteric students. In October, the annual meeting of the German Section of the Theosophical Society, which still remains very small, takes place. Rudolf Steiner reports membership has risen from 121 to 377 members. In November, seeking to establish esoteric 'continuity,' Rudolf Steiner and Marie von Sivers participate in a 'Memphis-Misraim' Masonic ceremony. They pay 45 marks for membership. 'Yesterday, you saw how little remains of former esoteric institutions.' 'We are dealing only with a "framework" . . for the present, nothing lies behind it. The occult powers have completely withdrawn.'

1906: Expansion of theosophical work. Rudolf Steiner gives about 245 lectures, only 44 of which take place in Berlin. Cycles are given in Paris, Leipzig, Stuttgart, and Munich. Esoteric work also intensifies. Rudolf Steiner begins writing *An Outline of Esoteric Science* (CW 13). In January, Rudolf Steiner receives permission (a patent) from the Great Orient of the Scottish A & A Thirty-Three Degree Rite of the Order of the Ancient Freemasons of the Memphis-Misraim Rite to direct a chapter under the name 'Mystica Aeterna.' This will become the 'Cognitive-Ritual Section' (also called 'Misraim Service') of the Esoteric School. (See: *Freemasonry and Ritual Work: The Misraim Service,* CW 265.) During this time, Steiner also meets Albert Schweitzer. In May, he is in Paris, where he visits Édouard Schuré. Many Russians attend his lectures (including Konstantin Balmont, Dimitri Mereszkovski, Zinaida Hippius, and Maximilian Woloshin). He attends the General Meeting of the European Federation of the Theosophical Society, at which Col. Olcott is present for the last time. He spends the year's end in Venice and Rome, where he writes and works on his translation of H.P. Blavatsky's *Key to Theosophy.*

1907: Further expansion of the German Theosophical Movement according to the Rosicrucian directive to 'introduce spirit into the world'—in education, in social questions, in art, and in science. In February, Col. Olcott dies in Adyar. Before he dies, Olcott indicates that 'the Masters' wish Annie Besant to succeed him: much politicking ensues. Rudolf Steiner supports Besant's candidacy. April–May: preparations for the Congress of the Federation of European Sections of the Theosophical Society—the great, watershed Whitsun 'Munich Congress,' attended by Annie Besant and others. Steiner decides to separate Eastern and Western (Christian–Rosicrucian) esoteric schools. He takes his esoteric school out of the Theosophical Society (Besant and Rudolf Steiner are 'in harmony' on this). Steiner makes his first lecture tours to Austria and Hungary. That summer, he is in Italy. In September, he visits Édouard Schuré, who will write the Introduction to the French edition of *Christianity as Mystical Fact* in Barr, Alsace. Rudolf Steiner writes the autobiographical statement known as the 'Barr Document.' In *Luzifer-Gnosis*, 'The Education of the Child' appears.

1908: The movement grows (membership: 1,150). Lecturing expands. Steiner makes his first extended lecture tour to Holland and Scandinavia, as well as visits to Naples and Sicily. Themes: St John's Gospel, the Apocalypse, Egypt, science, philosophy, and logic. *Luzifer-Gnosis* ceases publication. In Berlin, Marie von Sivers (with Johanna Mücke (1864–1949) forms the *Philosophisch-Theosophisch* (after 1915 *Philosophisch-Anthroposophisch) Verlag* to publish Steiner's work. Steiner gives lecture cycles titled *The Gospel of St John* (CW 103) and *The Apocalypse* (104).

1909: *An Outline of Esoteric Science* appears. Lecturing and travel continues. Rudolf Steiner's spiritual research expands to include the polarity of Lucifer and Ahriman; the work of great individualities in history; the Maitreya Buddha and the Bodhisattvas; spiritual economy (CW 109); the work of the spiritual hierarchies in heaven and on earth (CW 110). He also deepens and intensifies his research into the Gospels, giving lectures on the Gospel of St Luke (CW 114) with the first mention of two Jesus children. Meets and becomes friends with Christian Morgenstern (1871–1914). In April, he lays the foundation stone for the Malsch model—the building that will lead to the first Goetheanum. In May, the International Congress of the Federation of European Sections of the Theosophical Society takes place in Budapest. Rudolf Steiner receives the Subba Row medal for *How to Know Higher Worlds*. During this time, Charles W. Leadbeater discovers Jiddu Krishnamurti (1895–1986) and proclaims him the future 'world teacher,' the bearer of the Maitreya Buddha and the 'reappearing Christ.' In October, Steiner delivers seminal lectures on 'anthroposophy,' which he will try, unsuccessfully, to rework over the next years into the unfinished work, *Anthroposophy (A Fragment)* (CW 45).

1910: New themes: *The Reappearance of Christ in the Etheric* (CW 118); *The Fifth Gospel; The Mission of Folk Souls* (CW 121); *Occult History* (CW 126); the evolving development of etheric cognitive capacities. Rudolf Steiner continues his Gospel research with *The Gospel of St Matthew* (CW 123). In January, his father dies. In April, he takes a month-long trip to Italy, including Rome, Monte Cassino, and Sicily. He also visits Scandinavia again. July–August, he writes the first Mystery Drama, *The Portal of Initiation* (CW 14). In November, he gives 'psychosophy' lectures. In December, he submits 'On the

Psychological Foundations and Epistemological Framework of Theosophy' to the International Philosophical Congress in Bologna.

1911: The crisis in the Theosophical Society deepens. In January, 'The Order of the Rising Sun,' which will soon become 'The Order of the Star in the East,' is founded for the coming world teacher, Krishnamurti. At the same time, Marie von Sivers, Rudolf Steiner's co-worker, falls ill. Fewer lectures are given, but important new ground is broken. In Prague, in March, Steiner meets Franz Kafka (1883–1924) and Hugo Bergmann (1883–1975). In April, he delivers his paper to the Philosophical Congress. He writes the second Mystery Drama, *The Soul's Probation* (CW 14). Also, while Marie von Sivers is convalescing, Rudolf Steiner begins work on *Calendar 1912/1913*, which will contain the 'Calendar of the Soul' meditations. On March 19, Anna (Eunike) Steiner dies. In September, Rudolf Steiner visits Einsiedeln, birthplace of Paracelsus. In December, Friedrich Rittelmeyer, future founder of the Christian Community, meets Rudolf Steiner. The *Johannes-Bauverein,* the 'building committee,' which would lead to the first Goetheanum (first planned for Munich), is also founded, and a preliminary committee for the founding of an independent association is created that, in the following year, will become the Anthroposophical Society. Important lecture cycles include *Occult Physiology* (CW 128); *Wonders of the World* (CW 129); *From Jesus to Christ* (CW 131). Other themes: esoteric Christianity; Christian Rosenkreutz; the spiritual guidance of humanity; the sense world and the world of the spirit.

1912: Despite the ongoing, now increasing crisis in the Theosophical Society, much is accomplished: *Calendar 1912/1913* is published; eurythmy is created; both the third Mystery Drama, *The Guardian of the Threshold* (CW 14) and *A Way of Self-Knowledge* (CW 16) are written. New (or renewed) themes included life between death and rebirth and karma and reincarnation. Other lecture cycles: *Spiritual Beings in the Heavenly Bodies and in the Kingdoms of Nature* (CW 136); *The Human Being in the Light of Occultism, Theosophy, and Philosophy* (CW 137); *The Gospel of St Mark* (CW 139); and *The Bhagavad Gita and the Epistles of Paul* (CW 142). On May 8, Rudolf Steiner celebrates White Lotus Day, H.P. Blavatsky's death day, which he had faithfully observed for the past decade, for the last time. In August, Rudolf Steiner suggests the 'independent association' be called the 'Anthroposophical Society.' In September, the first eurythmy course takes place. In October, Rudolf Steiner declines recognition of a Theosophical Society lodge dedicated to the Star of the East and decides to expel all Theosophical Society members belonging to the order.

Also, with Marie von Sivers, he first visits Dornach, near Basel, Switzerland, and they stand on the hill where the Goetheanum will be built. In November, a Theosophical Society lodge is opened by direct mandate from Adyar (Annie Besant). In December, a meeting of the German section occurs at which it is decided that belonging to the Order of the Star of the East is incompatible with membership in the Theosophical Society. December 28: informal founding of the Anthroposophical Society in Berlin.

1913: Expulsion of the German section from the Theosophical Society. February 2–3: Foundation meeting of the Anthroposophical Society. Board members include: Marie von Sivers, Michael Bauer, and Carl Unger. September 20: Laying of the foundation stone for the *Johannes Bau* (Goetheanum) in Dornach. Building begins immediately. The fourth Mystery Drama, *The Soul's Awakening* (CW 14), is completed. Also: *The Threshold of the Spiritual World* (CW 147). Lecture cycles include: *The Bhagavad Gita and the Epistles of Paul* and *The Esoteric Meaning of the Bhagavad Gita* (CW 146), which the Russian philosopher Nikolai Berdyaev attends; *The Mysteries of the East and of Christianity* (CW 144); *The Effects of Esoteric Development* (CW 145); and *The Fifth Gospel* (CW 148). In May, Rudolf Steiner is in London and Paris, where anthroposophical work continues.

1914: Building continues on the *Johannes Bau* (Goetheanum) in Dornach, with artists and co-workers from seventeen nations. The general assembly of the Anthroposophical Society takes place. In May, Rudolf Steiner visits Paris, as well as Chartres Cathedral. June 28: assassination in Sarajevo ('Now the catastrophe has happened!'). August 1: War is declared. Rudolf Steiner returns to Germany from Dornach—he will travel back and forth. He writes the last chapter of *The Riddles of Philosophy*. Lecture cycles include: *Human and Cosmic Thought* (CW 151); *Inner Being of Humanity between Death and a New Birth* (CW 153); *Occult Reading and Occult Hearing* (CW 156). December 24: marriage of Rudolf Steiner and Marie von Sivers.

1915: Building continues. Life after death becomes a major theme, also art. Writes: *Thoughts during a Time of War* (CW 24). Lectures include: *The Secret of Death* (CW 159); *The Uniting of Humanity through the Christ Impulse* (CW 165).

1916: Rudolf Steiner begins work with Edith Maryon (1872–1924) on the sculpture 'The Representative of Humanity' ('The Group'—Christ, Lucifer, and Ahriman). He also works with the alchemist Alexander von Bernus on the quarterly *Das Reich*. He writes *The Riddle of Humanity* (CW 20). Lectures include: *Necessity and Freedom in World History and Human Action* (CW 166); *Past and Present in the*

Human Spirit (CW 167); *The Karma of Vocation* (CW 172); *The Karma of Untruthfulness* (CW 173).

1917: Russian Revolution. The U.S. enters the war. Building continues. Rudolf Steiner delineates the idea of the 'threefold nature of the human being' (in a public lecture March 15) and the 'threefold nature of the social organism' (hammered out in May–June with the help of Otto von Lerchenfeld and Ludwig Polzer-Hoditz in the form of two documents titled *Memoranda,* which were distributed in high places). August–September: Rudolf Steiner writes *The Riddles of the Soul* (CW 20). Also: commentary on 'The Chymical Wedding of Christian Rosenkreutz' for Alexander Bernus (Das *Reich*). Lectures include: *The Karma of Materialism* (CW 176); *The Spiritual Background of the Outer World: The Fall of the Spirits of Darkness* (CW 177).

1918: March 18: peace treaty of Brest-Litovsk—'Now everything will truly enter chaos! What is needed is cultural renewal.' June: Rudolf Steiner visits Karlstein (Grail) Castle outside Prague. Lecture cycle: *From Symptom to Reality in Modern History* (CW 185). In mid-November, Emil Molt, of the Waldorf-Astoria Cigarette Company, has the idea of founding a school for his workers' children.

1919: Focus on the threefold social organism: tireless travel, countless lectures, meetings, and publications. At the same time, a new public stage of Anthroposophy emerges as cultural renewal begins. The coming years will see initiatives in pedagogy, medicine, pharmacology, and agriculture. January 27: threefold meeting: 'We must first of all, with the money we have, found free schools that can bring people what they need.' February: first public eurythmy performance in Zurich. Also: 'Appeal to the German People' (CW 24), circulated March 6 as a newspaper insert. In April, *Towards Social Renewal* (CW 23) appears—'perhaps the most widely read of all books on politics appearing since the war'. Rudolf Steiner is asked to undertake the 'direction and leadership' of the school founded by the Waldorf-Astoria Company. Rudolf Steiner begins to talk about the 'renewal' of education. May 30: a building is selected and purchased for the future Waldorf School. August–September, Rudolf Steiner gives a lecture course for Waldorf teachers, *The Foundations of Human Experience (Study of Man)* (CW 293). September 7: Opening of the first Waldorf School. December (into January): first science course, the *Light Course* (CW 320).

1920: The Waldorf School flourishes. New threefold initiatives. Founding of limited companies *Der Kommende Tag* and *Futurum A.G.* to infuse spiritual values into the economic realm. Rudolf Steiner also focuses on the sciences. Lectures: *Introducing Anthroposophical*

Medicine (CW 312); *The Warmth Course* (CW 321); *The Boundaries of Natural Science* (CW 322); *The Redemption of Thinking* (CW 74). February: Johannes Werner Klein—later a co-founder of the Christian Community—asks Rudolf Steiner about the possibility of a 'religious renewal,' a 'Johannine church.' In March, Rudolf Steiner gives the first course for doctors and medical students. In April, a divinity student asks Rudolf Steiner a second time about the possibility of religious renewal. September 27–October 16: anthroposophical 'university course.' December: lectures titled *The Search for the New Isis* (CW 202).

1921: Rudolf Steiner continues his intensive work on cultural renewal, including the uphill battle for the threefold social order. 'University' arts, scientific, theological, and medical courses include: *The Astronomy Course* (CW 323); *Observation, Mathematics, and Scientific Experiment* (CW 324); the *Second Medical Course* (CW 313); *Colour.* In June and September–October, Rudolf Steiner also gives the first two 'priests' courses' (CW 342 and 343). The 'youth movement' gains momentum. Magazines are founded: *Die Drei* (January), and—under the editorship of Albert Steffen (1884–1963)—the weekly, *Das Goetheanum* (August). In February–March, Rudolf Steiner takes his first trip outside Germany since the war (Holland). On April 7, Steiner receives a letter regarding 'religious renewal,' and May 22–23, he agrees to address the question in a practical way. In June, the Klinical-Therapeutic Institute opens in Arlesheim under the direction of Dr Ita Wegman. In August, the Chemical-Pharmaceutical Laboratory opens in Arlesheim (Oskar Schmiedel and Ita Wegman are directors). The Clinical Therapeutic Institute is inaugurated in Stuttgart (Dr Ludwig Noll is director); also the Research Laboratory in Dornach (Ehrenfried Pfeiffer and Gunther Wachsmuth are directors). In November–December, Rudolf Steiner visits Norway.

1922: The first half of the year involves very active public lecturing (thousands attend); in the second half, Rudolf Steiner begins to withdraw and turn toward the Society—'The Society is asleep.' It is 'too weak' to do what is asked of it. The businesses—*Der Kommende Tag* and *Futurum A.G.*—fail. In January, with the help of an agent, Steiner undertakes a twelve-city German lecture tour, accompanied by eurythmy performances. In two weeks he speaks to more than 2,000 people. In April, he gives a 'university course' in The Hague. He also visits England. In June, he is in Vienna for the East–West Congress. In August–September, he is back in England for the Oxford Conference on Education. Returning to Dornach, he gives the lectures *Philosophy, Cosmology, and Religion*

(CW 215), and gives the third priests' course (CW 344). On September 16, The Christian Community is founded. In October–November, Steiner is in Holland and England. He also speaks to the youth: *The Youth Course* (CW 217). In December, Steiner gives lectures titled *The Origins of Natural Science* (CW 326), and *Humanity and the World of Stars: The Spiritual Communion of Humanity* (CW 219). December 31: Fire at the Goetheanum, which is destroyed.

1923: Despite the fire, Rudolf Steiner continues his work unabated. A very hard year. Internal dispersion, dissension, and apathy abound. There is conflict—between old and new visions—within the Society. A wake-up call is needed, and Rudolf Steiner responds with renewed lecturing vitality. His focus: the spiritual context of human life; initiation science; the course of the year; and community building. As a foundation for an artistic school, he creates a series of pastel sketches. Lecture cycles: *The Anthroposophical Movement; Initiation Science* (CW 227) (in Wales at the Penmaenmawr Summer School); *The Four Seasons and the Archangels* (CW 229); *Harmony of the Creative Word* (CW 230); *The Supersensible Human* (CW 231), given in Holland for the founding of the Dutch society. On November 10, in response to the failed Hitler-Ludendorff putsch in Munich, Steiner closes his Berlin residence and moves the *Philosophisch-Anthroposophisch Verlag* (Press) to Dornach. On December 9, Steiner begins the serialization of his *Autobiography: The Course of My Life* (CW 28) in *Das Goetheanum*. It will continue to appear weekly, without a break, until his death. Late December–early January: Rudolf Steiner re-founds the Anthroposophical Society (about 12,000 members internationally) and takes over its leadership. The new board members are: Marie Steiner, Ita Wegman, Albert Steffen, Elisabeth Vreede, and Gunther Wachsmuth. (See *The Christmas Meeting for the Founding of the General Anthroposophical Society*, CW 260.) Accompanying lectures: *Mystery Knowledge and Mystery Centres* (CW 232); *World History in the Light of Anthroposophy* (CW 233). December 25: the Foundation Stone is laid (in the hearts of members) in the form of the 'Foundation Stone Meditation.'

1924: January 1: having founded the Anthroposophical Society and taken over its leadership, Rudolf Steiner has the task of 'reforming' it. The process begins with a weekly newssheet ('What's Happening in the Anthroposophical Society') in which Rudolf Steiner's 'Letters to Members' and 'Anthroposophical Leading Thoughts' appear (CW 26). The next step is the creation of a new esoteric class, the 'first class' of the 'University of Spiritual Science' (which was to have been followed, had Rudolf Steiner lived longer, by two more advanced classes). Then comes a new language for

Anthroposophy—practical, phenomenological, and direct; and Rudolf Steiner creates the model for the second Goetheanum. He begins the series of extensive 'karma' lectures (CW 235–40); and finally, responding to needs, he creates two new initiatives: biodynamic agriculture and curative education. After the middle of the year, rumours begin to circulate regarding Steiner's health. Lectures: January–February, *Anthroposophy* (CW 234); February: *Tone Eurythmy* (CW 278); June: *The Agriculture Course* (CW 327); June–July: *Speech Eurythmy* (CW 279); *Curative Education* (CW 317); August: (England, 'Second International Summer School'), *Initiation Consciousness: True and False Paths in Spiritual Investigation* (CW 243); September: *Pastoral Medicine* (CW 318). On September 26, for the first time, Rudolf Steiner cancels a lecture. On September 28, he gives his last lecture. On September 29, he withdraws to his studio in the carpenter's shop; now he is definitively ill. Cared for by Ita Wegman, he continues working, however, and writing the weekly installments of his *Autobiography* and *Letters to the Members/Leading Thoughts* (CW 26).

1925: Rudolf Steiner, while continuing to work, continues to weaken. He finishes *Extending Practical Medicine* (CW 27) with Ita Wegman. On March 30, around ten in the morning, Rudolf Steiner dies.

INDEX

B

C

D

E

I

J

R

S

Z